PHOTOGRAPHER'S AMERICA

Utah Unique

Nick Bagley

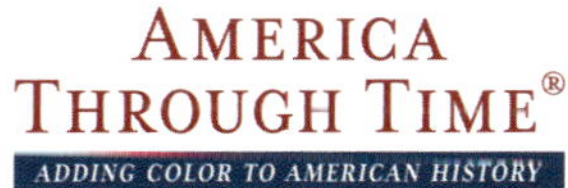

Dedicated to the explorers, artists, and dreamers who are reading this book. Without you, this wouldn't be possible. Now let's get on with it!

America Through Time is an imprint of Fonthill Media LLC
www.through-time.com
office@through-time.com

Published by Arcadia Publishing by arrangement with Fonthill Media LLC
For all general information, please contact Arcadia Publishing:
Telephone: 843-853-2070
Fax: 843-853-0044
E-mail: sales@arcadiapublishing.com
For customer service and orders:
Toll-Free 1-888-313-2665

www.arcadiapublishing.com

First published 2022

ISBN 978-1-63499-378-4

Typeset in Gotham Book
Printed and bound in England

Contents

About the Author

Nick Bagley is an author and photographer who enjoys exploring strange and mysterious places. Born in New York and now residing in Salt Lake City, Nick adventures to forgotten locations all over the country. His passion for photography and interest in history allows him to create a visually stunning window into the past. Through his books and social media, Nick presents his following with visually pleasing images combined with interesting stories and facts. For Nick, every adventure brings new challenges and excitement, and every photo represents an extension of his take on our ever-changing world.

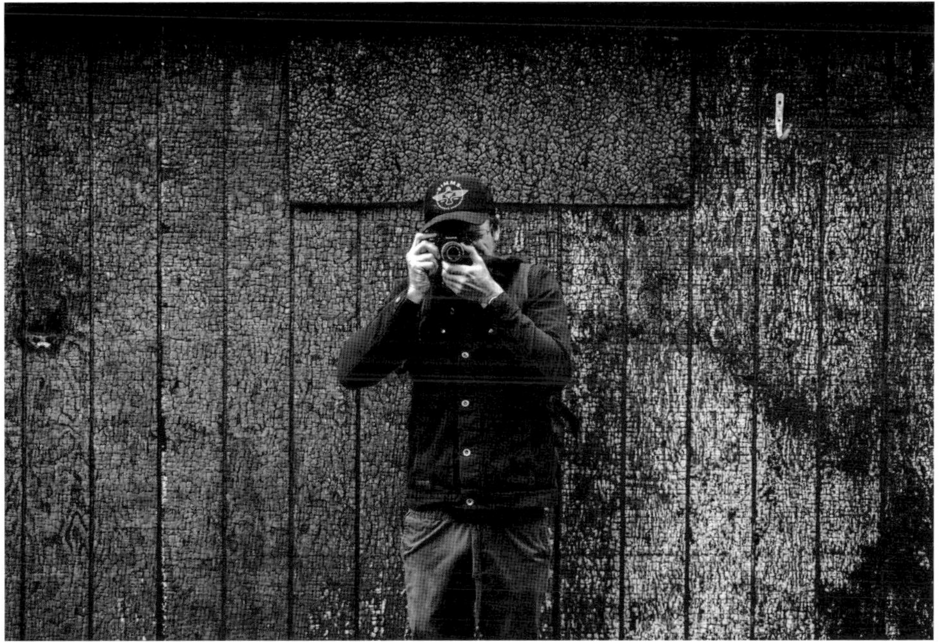

Introduction

The view of our world varies greatly. Specific feelings and thoughts can be triggered by objects and locations, and I've made it my goal to hunt down these triggers. In my case, I like off-the-beaten-path and unique areas: some are weird, some are utterly terrifying, and others are just plain cool. Before you lies a collection of words and photographs that showcase Utah through my eyes.

Hidden deep within the words lies a map; use it to help you on your own adventure. While this may be from my point of view, I encourage all of my readers to go out and explore. Fans of my first book, *Abandoned Utah*, know that my tastes lie in the dark and often unknown areas of the state. This book is no different, focusing mainly on Salt Lake City (but touching on a few other places).

1

Cemetery

Hidden amongst the headstones of the 120-acre Salt Lake City cemetery lies a unique grave, marked Lilly E. Gray, June 6, 1881–Nov 14, 1958. Victim of the Beast 666." It is a genuinely ominous headstone that immediately attracted my attention. When I visited, the aftermath of a recent windstorm was apparent. Massive trees had been toppled, causing their roots to tear open gravesites. Headstones were strewn about the property. But Lilly's grave was untouched. I wondered why her epitaph was so dark and mysterious. What had happened to Lilly? Was she murdered? Did she worship Satan? Asking around I couldn't find much information. So, I dove a little deeper.

Lilly had been born in Canada in 1898 and didn't find herself in Salt Lake City until 1950. Marriage records show that Lilly married Elmer Gray roughly two years after she arrived. It is uncertain how Lilly and Elmer met, but it is speculated that they had worked together. Elmer's past was filled with crime. Being in and out of jail for most of his life, Elmer was finally released and went clean. He had spent ten years and six months in prison after being caught breaking into the Kamas Confectionery building. At the time of his release in 1948, Elmer was sixty-seven years old.

Lilly and Elmer tied the knot in 1950. Records show nothing out of the ordinary occurred between then and the time of her death in 1958. I could find zero evidence of any devil worship or anything else that would contribute to her epitaph. Death records show that Lilly died of kidney failure and pulmonary embolism. She wasn't murdered. Elmer decided what would go on her headstone, and it seems Elmer is the only one who knew the truth behind its meaning.

Adding more creepiness to the story, Elmer died on Halloween night in 1964. To this day, no one knows why Elmer decided on those words for Lilly's headstone. Some speculate that it was his strange way of showing his hatred towards society. After all, he was a criminal for the majority of his life. Other people think that his Parkinson's disease may have been a factor. Tremors, delusions, and hallucinations are all symptoms of this disease. His death certificate confirms he had the disease when he passed. Was he hallucinating when he wrote the epitaph? Or could it have an evil meaning? Either way, only Elmer will ever know the truth. The truth he took to his grave.

We don't have to go far to find our next item of interest. In the same cemetery lies another mysterious grave, that of Jacob Moritz. Legends say that if you walk around it three times, holding a candle, while chanting the words "emo, emo, emo," glowing red eyes will appear. Although you can still visit and walk around the grave, the window that once showcased the broken urn of ashes is now blocked to the public by a metal plate. Who started this legend? Did Jacob Moritz have a mysterious death causing him to haunt his grave forever? Why is the word "emo" the key to his conjuring? With a little bit of digging, here's what I was able to find out.

Born in Bavaria in 1849, Jacob Moritz immigrated to the United States when he turned 17. He lived in New York before eventually moving to Helena, Montana. Moritz moved to Utah in 1875 where he opened his first brewery. Moritz named his first brewery the Little Montana Brewery. After several years he found success, and even bought a stake in other breweries. In 1881, he opened a brand-new brewery, the Salt Lake Brewing Company.

With award-winning beer, Moritzs' wealth kept growing. His brewery expanded to a capacity of 6,000 bottles a day. He also owned and operated thirty-six saloons all over Utah. Wealth brought influence and he soon found himself involved with local politics. Despite being involved with alcohol production, the local Mormon population graciously accepted him into their society. He was a charitable man and regularly donated to various organizations.

In 1909, Moritz fell ill. He left Utah with his wife, hopeful that a change of scenery and air would improve his illness. Unfortunately, Moritz died six months later of stomach cancer. His ashes were placed inside a monument in the Salt Lake City Cemetery.

I could find no mention of the word emo or anything relating to the legend in Moritz's past. As far as I could tell, he had lived an honest and successful life. Yet, the legend remains as strong as ever. Of course, there's always the possibility that Moritz wasn't so honest. Maybe some hidden trauma or dark deed has bound him forever to this earth. Either way, I encourage you to see for yourself. Walk around the grave three times and chant the words, "emo, emo, emo." If you're lucky (or unlucky), Moritz may pay you a visit, his red eyes staring into your soul.

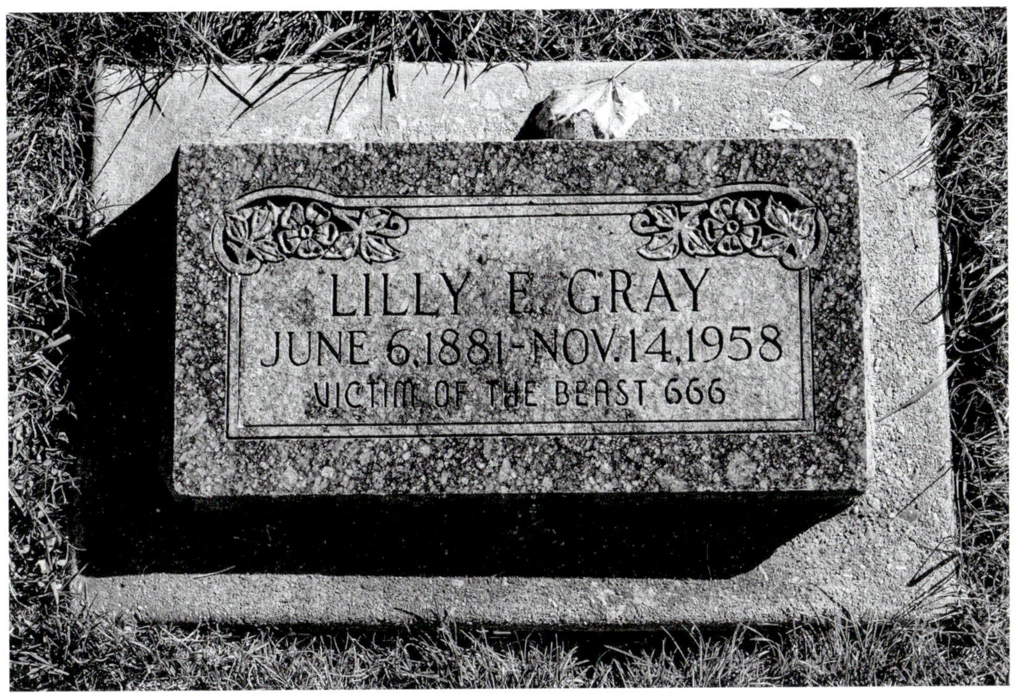

Mark of the Beast 666.

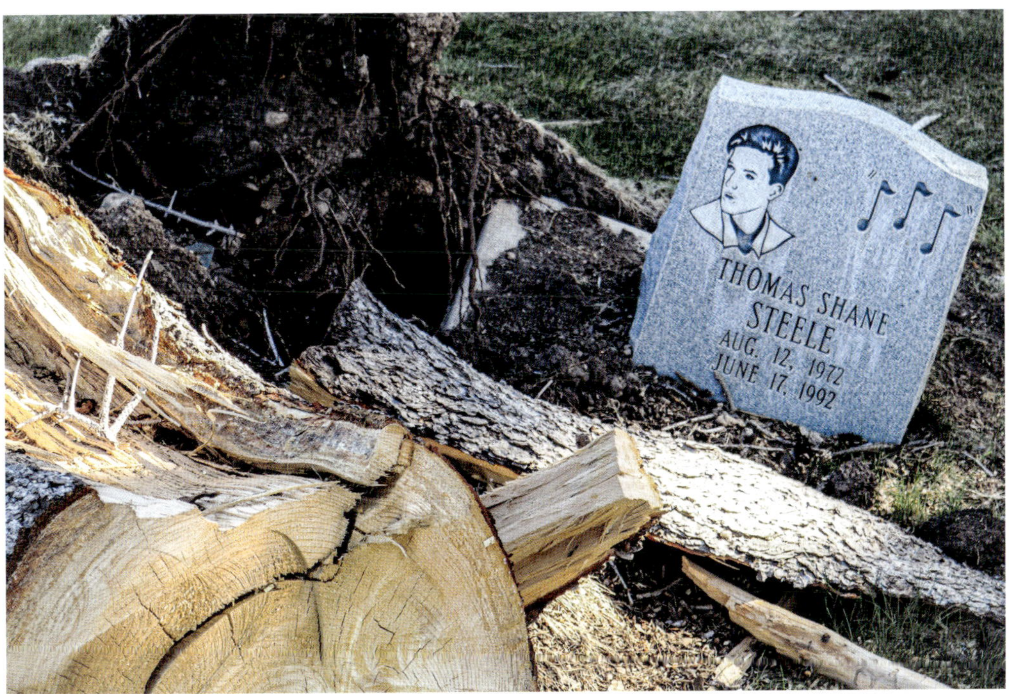

A recent windstorm had done severe damage to parts of the cemetery. Gravestones had been elevated and strewn about from tree roots being ripped from the ground.

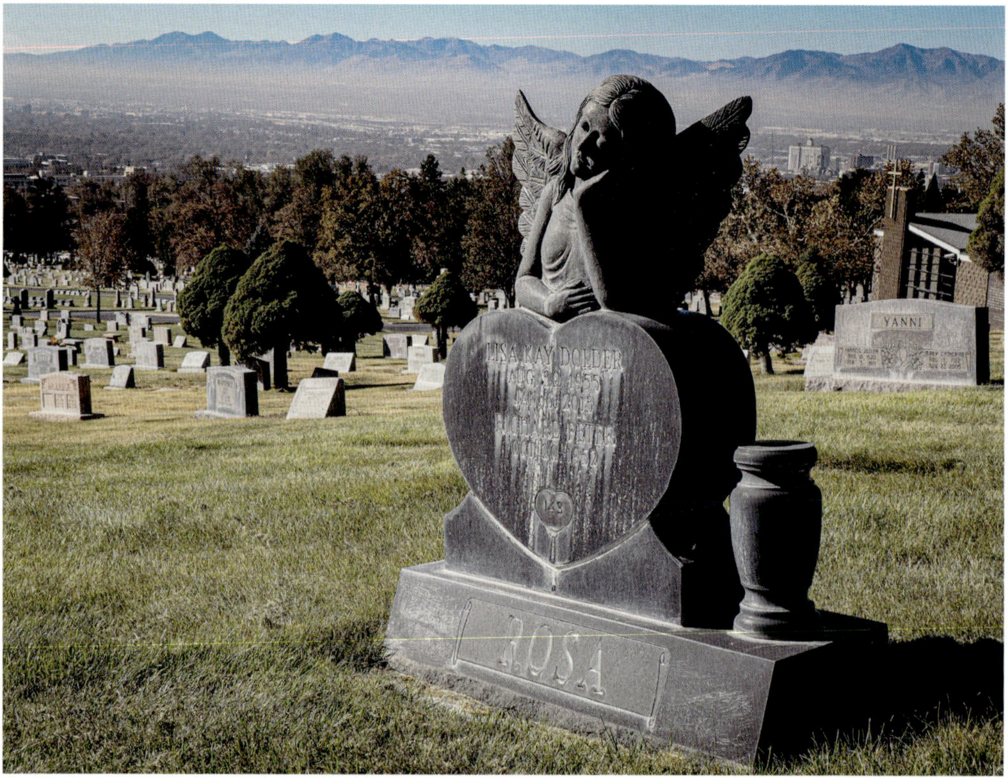

Rosa.

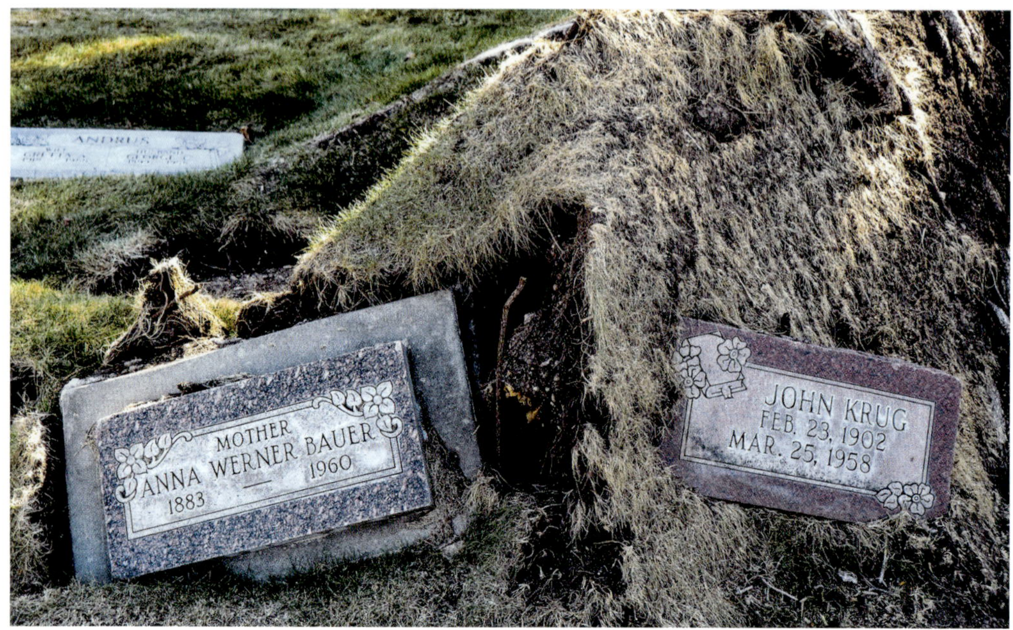

Did they escape their dark dwellings? No, just more storm damage.

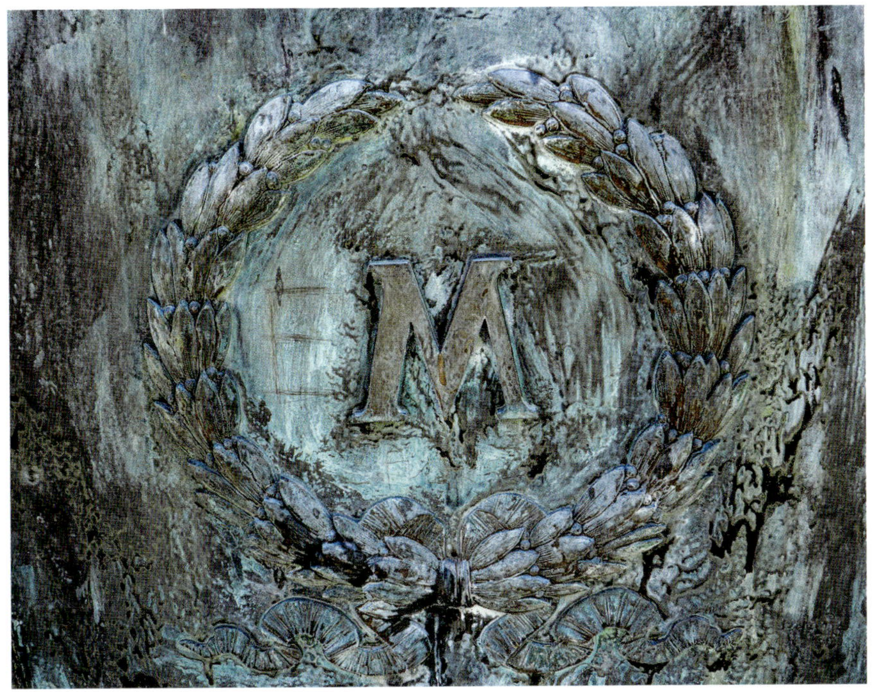

Emo.

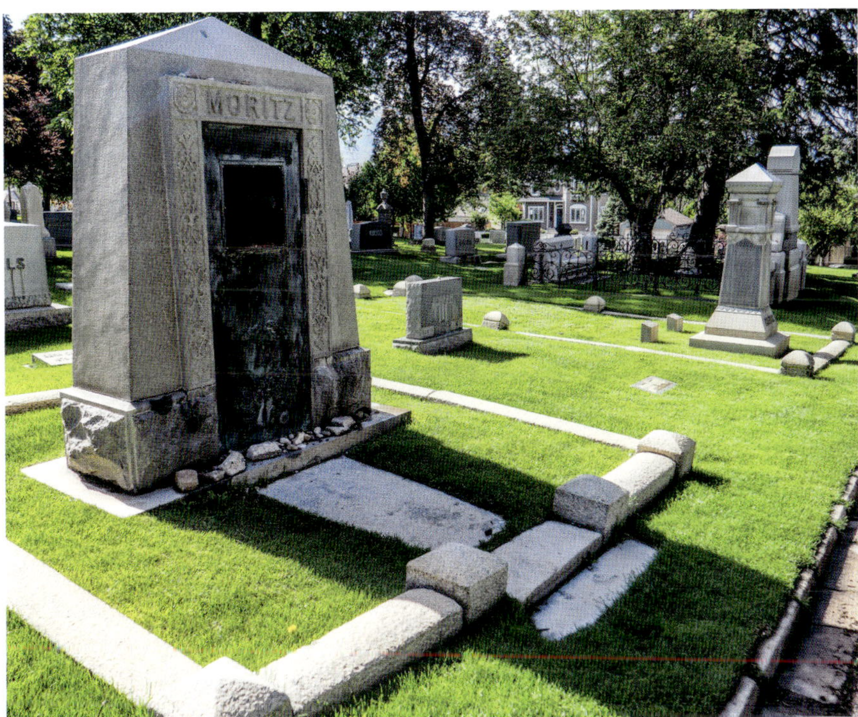

The Legendary Moritz gravestone looms within the Salt Lake Cemetery.

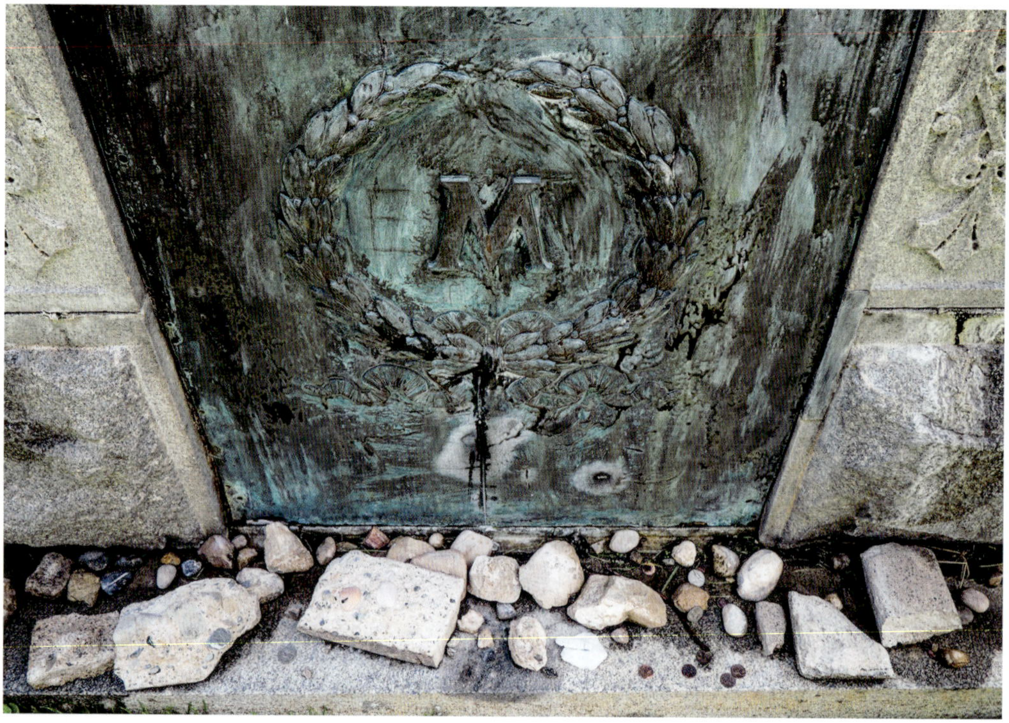

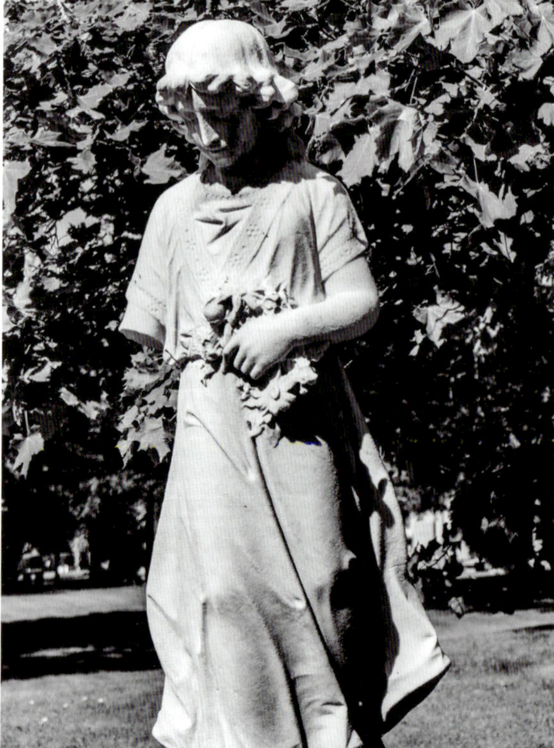

Above: Rocks are regularly placed on the grave, a sign of remembrance.

Left: Statues in various states of decay surround the old gravesites.

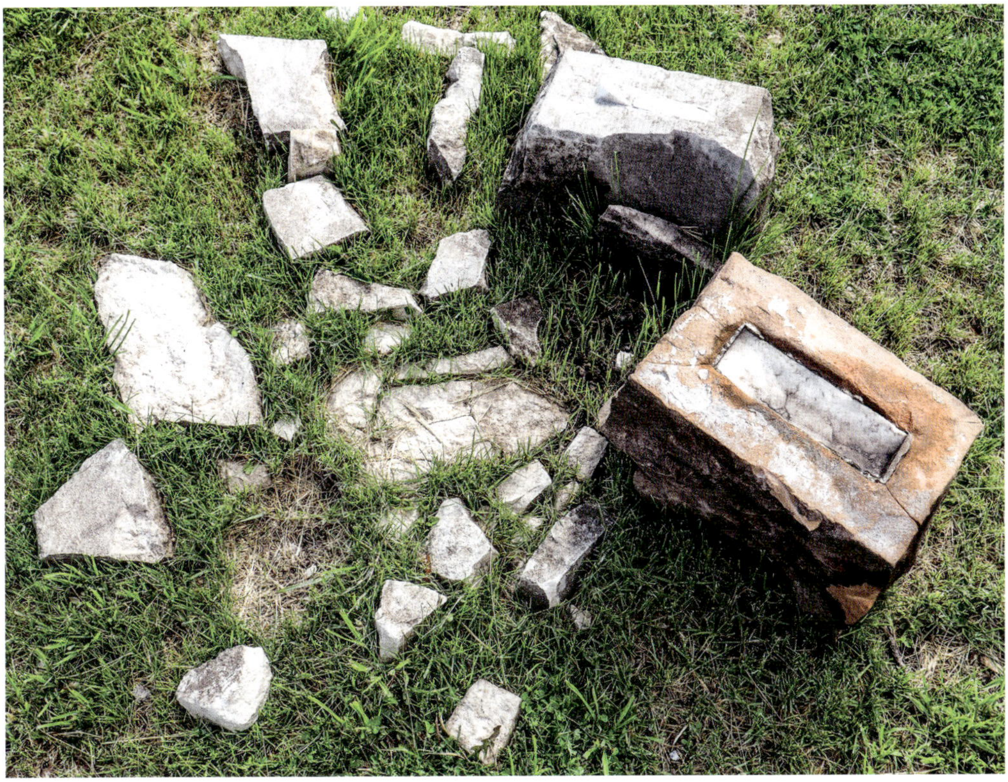

Some gravesites are so old that their headstones have fallen apart. Most likely for a child, this small headstone lies in multiple pieces.

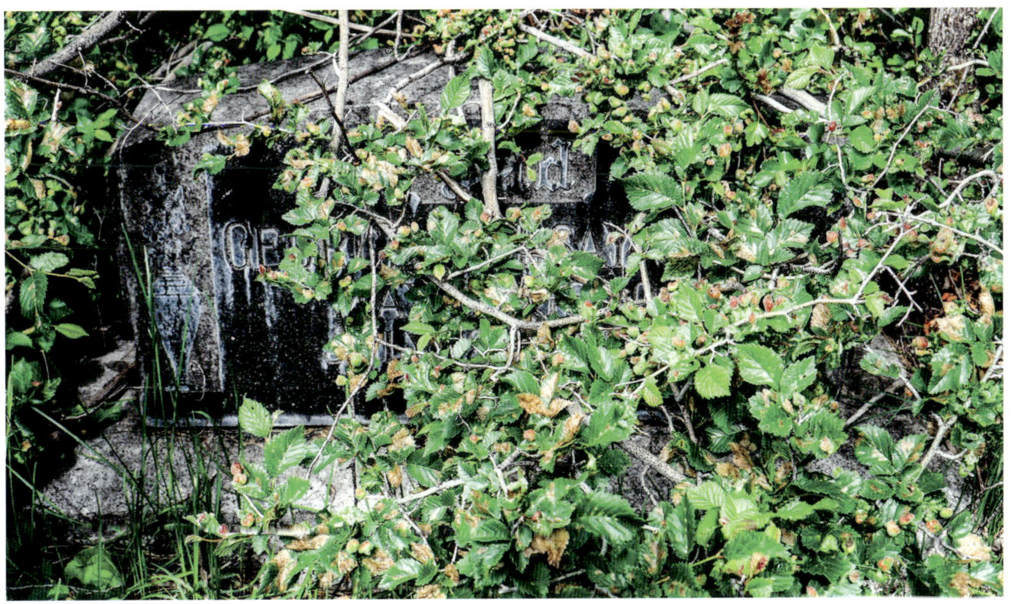

Some of the older sections of the cemetery have become overgrown.

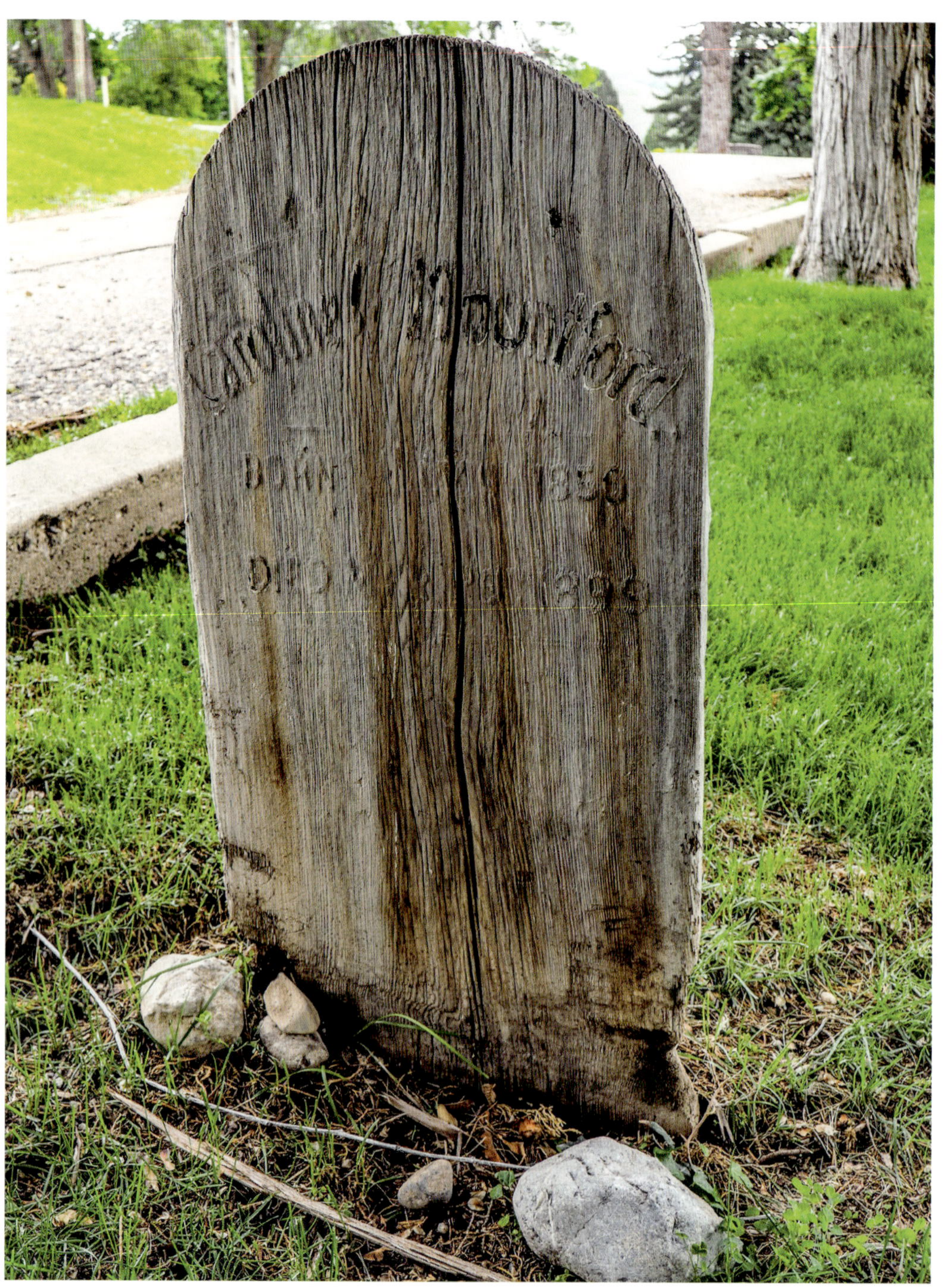

Some wood gravesite markers surprisingly remain, like this one dating back to the late 1800s.

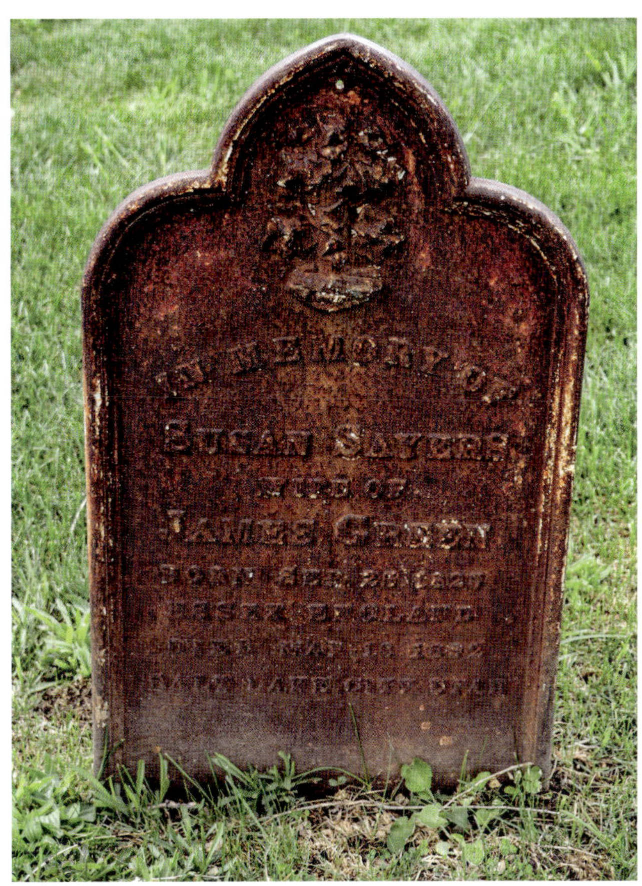

Susan.

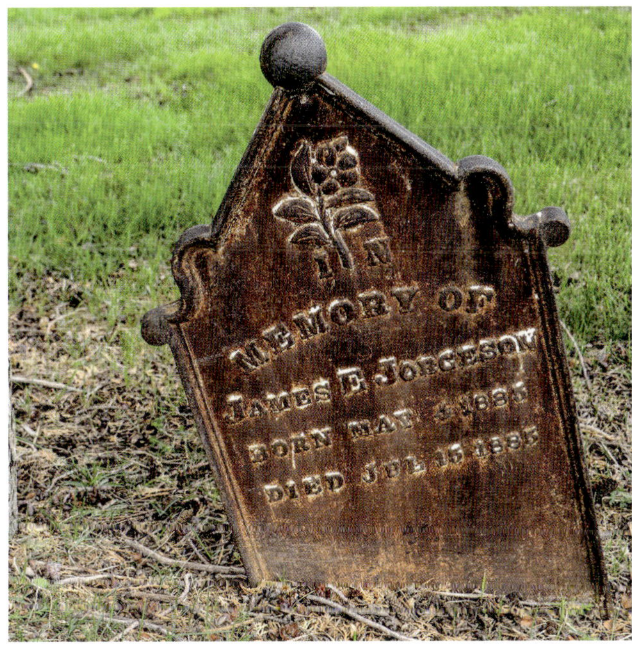

Worn metal gravemarker.

2

McCune Mansion

A hauntingly mysterious mansion sits atop the hillside overlooking downtown Salt Lake City. It seems out of place in this day and age. Its dark beauty still fills the soul with a sense of wonder. Designed by Alfred W. McCune and his wife, Elizabeth, the mansion was completed in 1901, costing roughly $1,000,000. The McCune family found their way to Salt Lake City when Alfred was just a small child. Alfred was born at a British Military base in India. Alfred's father decided to move to Salt Lake City after being persuaded by Mormon missionaries.

Initially, the McCune family settled in Nephi, Utah. Although not poor by any means, Alfred found himself working at a young age as a sheepherder. By the age of nineteen, Alfred had moved out of the house and started working for the Union Pacific Railroad. It was here that he learned the ins and outs of industry and business. Shortly thereafter, he opened a general store and sold lumber contracts to the railroad. Alfred had his hands in all different types of business over his life, which led to him becoming one of the first millionaires in Utah.

Alfred regularly invested in the infrastructure of Salt Lake City. At one point, he owned nearly one-third of Salt Lake's trolley system. He pushed for the trolley system to be all electric, creating the basis for the electric trains that run through the city today. Being heavily involved in local politics, he twice ran for office. He was unsuccessful both times, and after his second loss in 1920, he moved away from Salt Lake City for good. The house was donated to the LDS Church in 1921, and the building became officially known as the McCune School for Music and Arts.

In 1957, the McCune School had officially ended. It was then turned into the Brigham Young University Salt Lake City Center. By 1972, the center moved to a more prominent location. Eventually, the mansion turned into the Virginia Tanner School of Modern Dance. The school thrived for roughly two decades, until it too moved out in the early 1990s. Eighty years of wear and tear had begun to show on the mansion. Its future was now uncertain. To make things worse, the building had received damage from the 1999 Salt Lake City tornado. Fortunately, the estate was purchased later that year by the McCarthy family. They saved and restored the beautiful mansion back to its former glory.

Considering how many lives have passed throughout the house over the years, it's no wonder so many visitors have had paranormal experiences. Ghostly activity was first mentioned when the music school moved into the house. Students and visitors had heard organ music playing in the drawing-room when the house was empty. Whispers and disembodied voices were commonly heard throughout the house as well. Doors opened and closed at will, even if they had been locked.

On the first floor, facing the west wall, a small girl has been seen walking in and out of a mirror. Her footprints have been found all over the mansion as well. She seems to prefer weddings and parties, often re-arranging tables and flowers. Guests have photographed her on several occasions. A male entity has been seen wandering the house wearing dark clothing and a cape. Some speculate that this figure is the ghost of Mr. McCune himself. The son of Phil McCarthy told his dad that he had met this strange dark figure while he was in the mansion alone. The figure appeared before him, watched him for a few moments, and suddenly disappeared. This same figure was attributed with turning the lights off and on in the ballroom during a Christmas celebration. The caretaker of the house had discovered a hidden light switch located two floors below the ballroom. Some speculate that the ghost of Mr. McCune had been turning the lights off and on.

Presently the mansion can be rented for parties, weddings, and other private events. If you call ahead, Preservation Utah will schedule a tour (depending on current pandemic restrictions). The McCune Mansion is well worth the visit for tourists and locals alike. Just be sure to be respectful of the property, for you never know what the spirits may do if you are not.

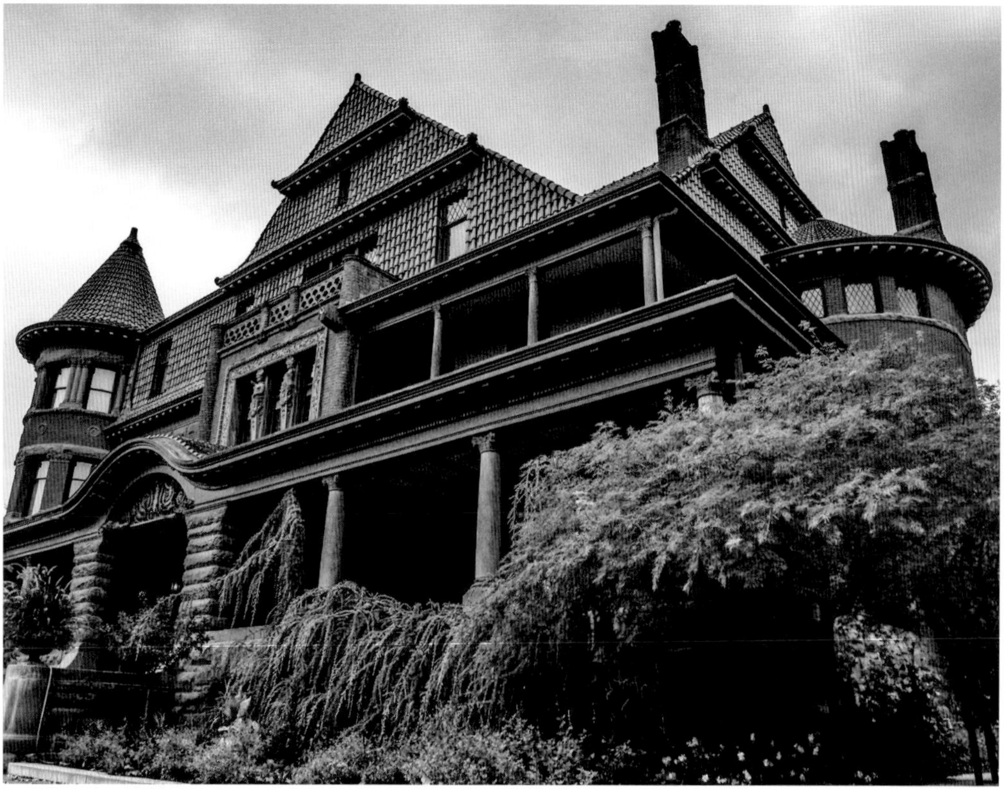

The McCune Mansion looms atop the hillside watching the city below.

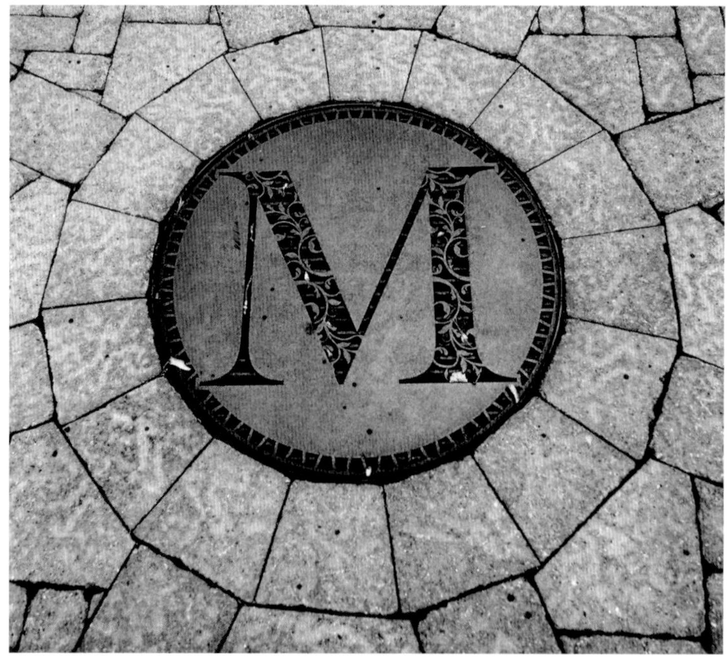

An "M" marking the center of the driveway.

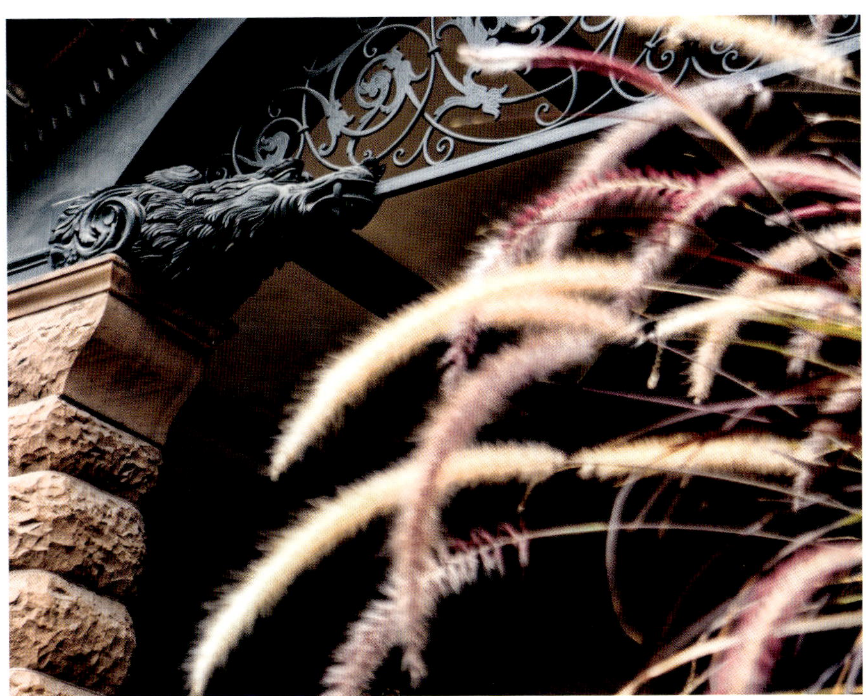

Wildlife through the shrubs.

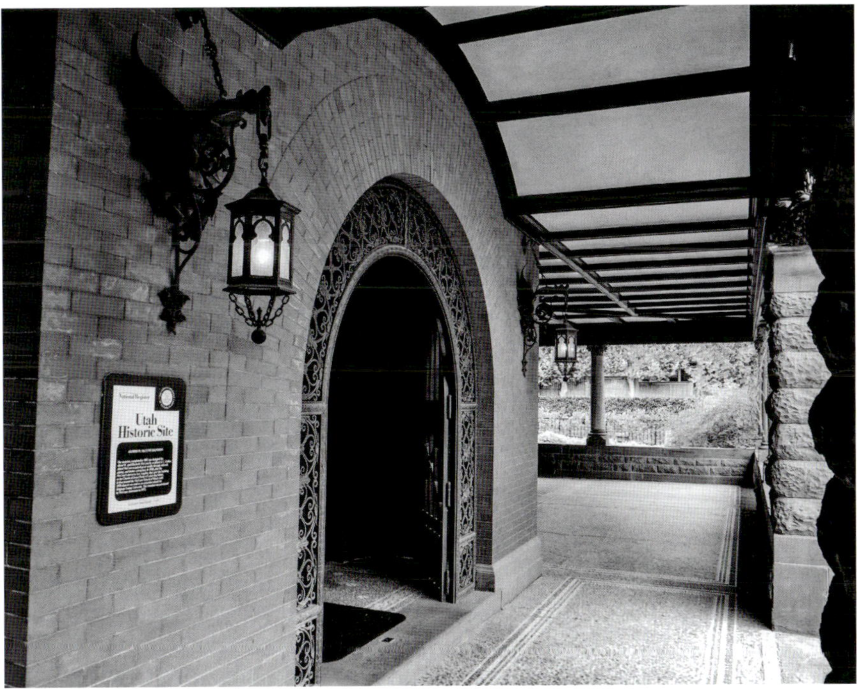

Usually open to the public for tours and events, the mansion was shut down due to the pandemic. Reach out to Preservation Utah for more information.

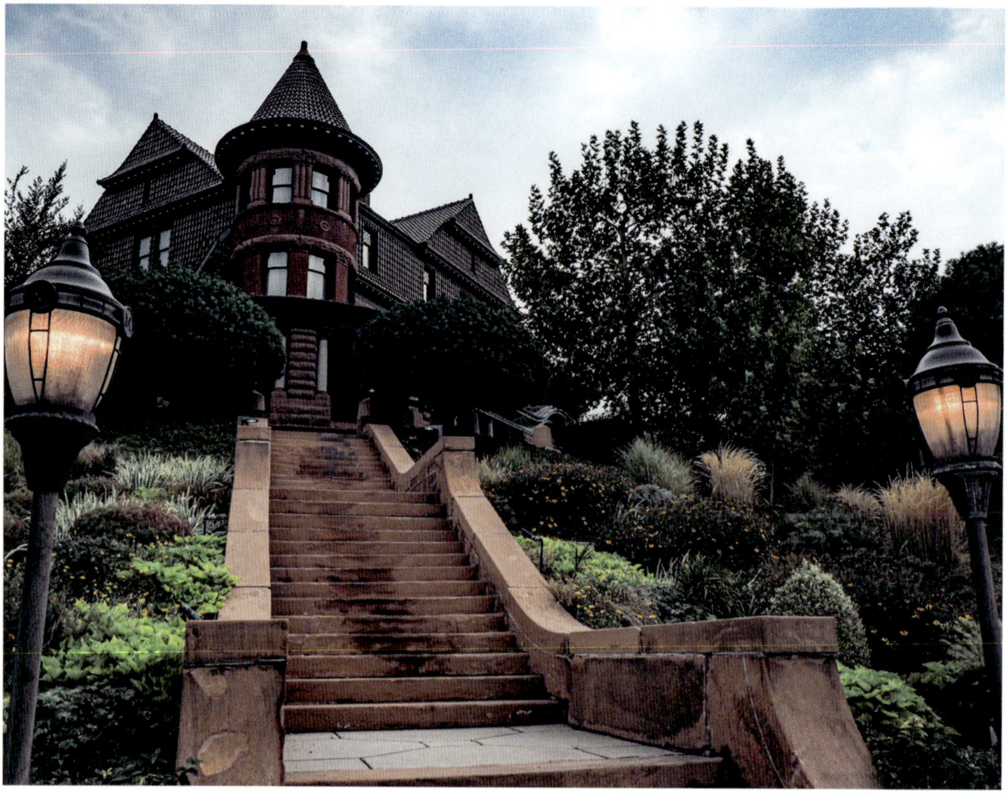

The long staircase to the entrance beckons visitors to explore its grounds.

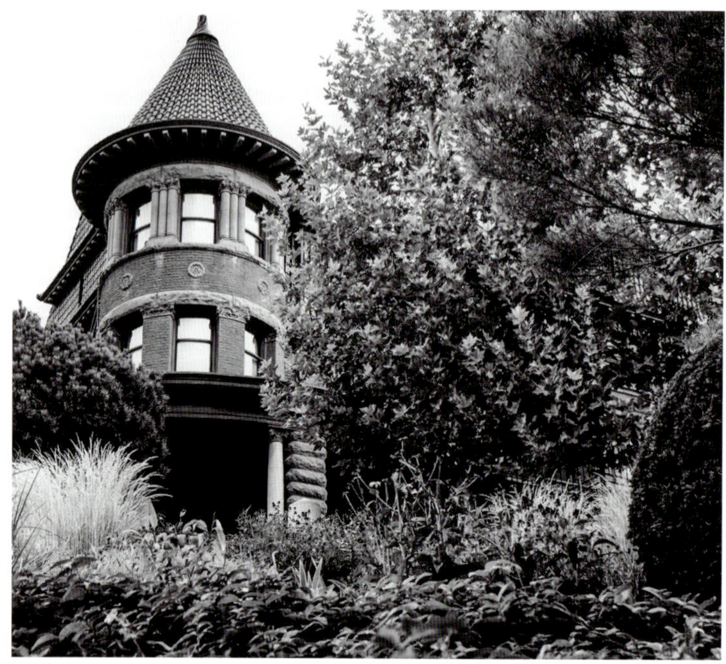

A well-maintained garden and courtyard fill the property with lush foliage.

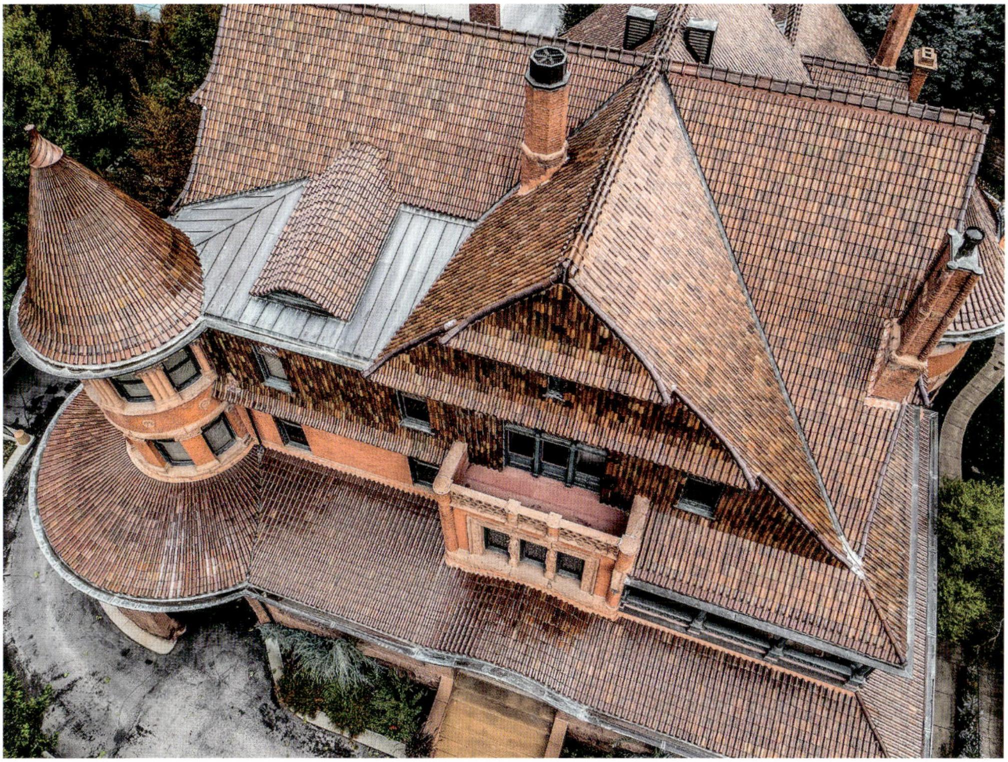

A birdseye view showcases the vibrant brick red color of the property.

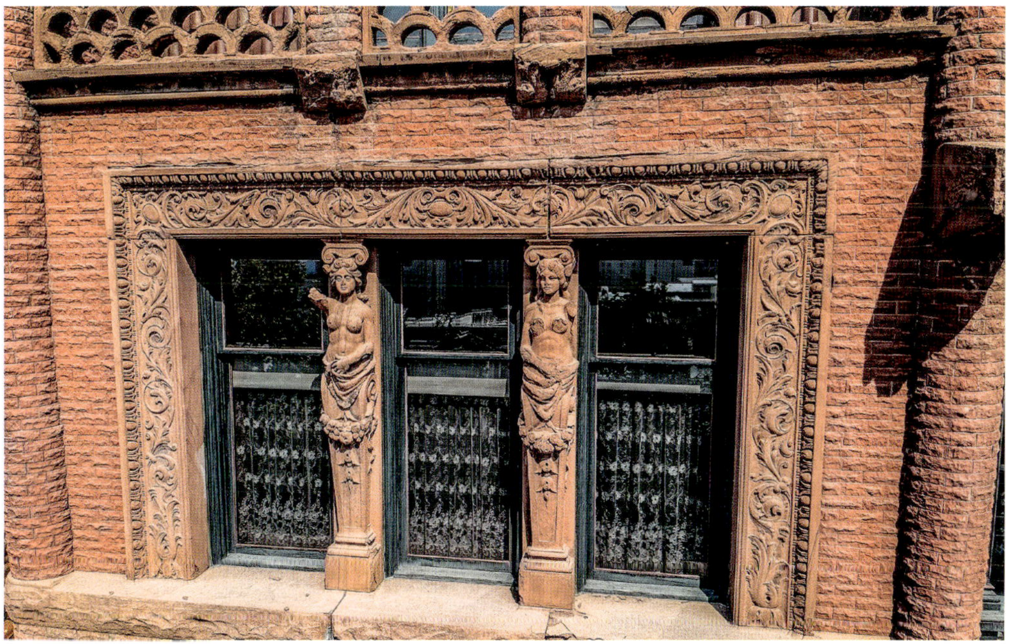

Ornate stonework can be found hidden within the architecture.

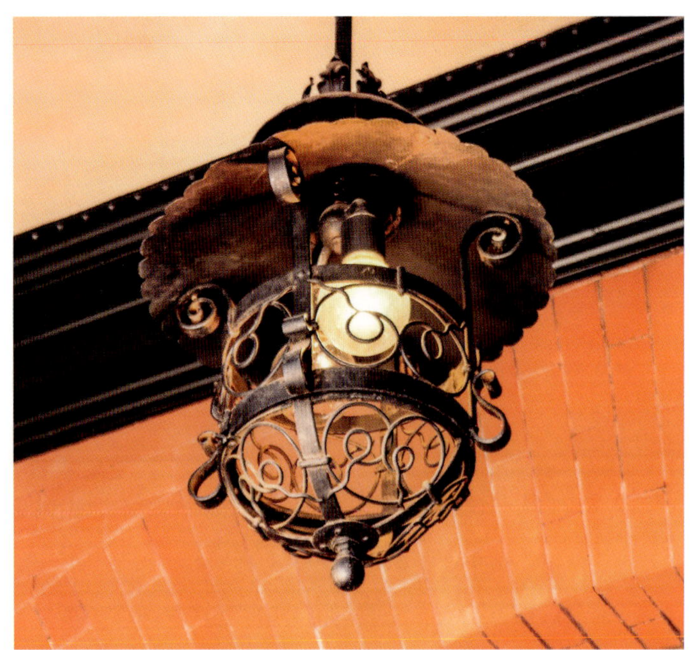

The mansion has been beautifully restored.

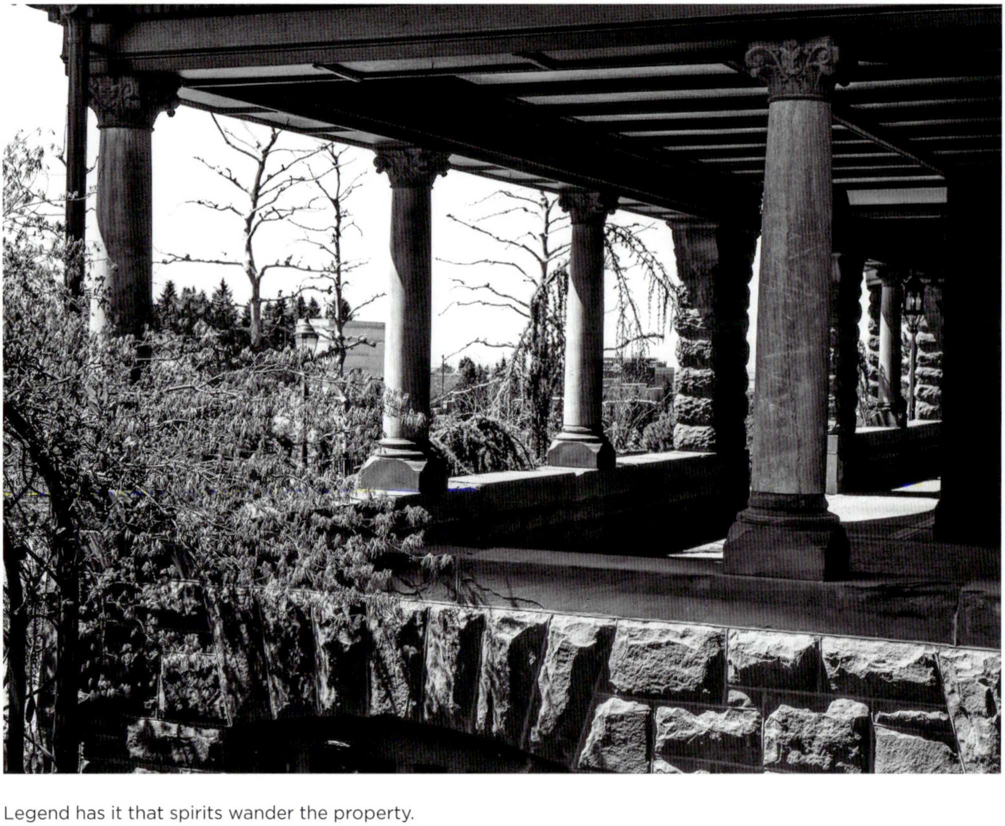

Legend has it that spirits wander the property.

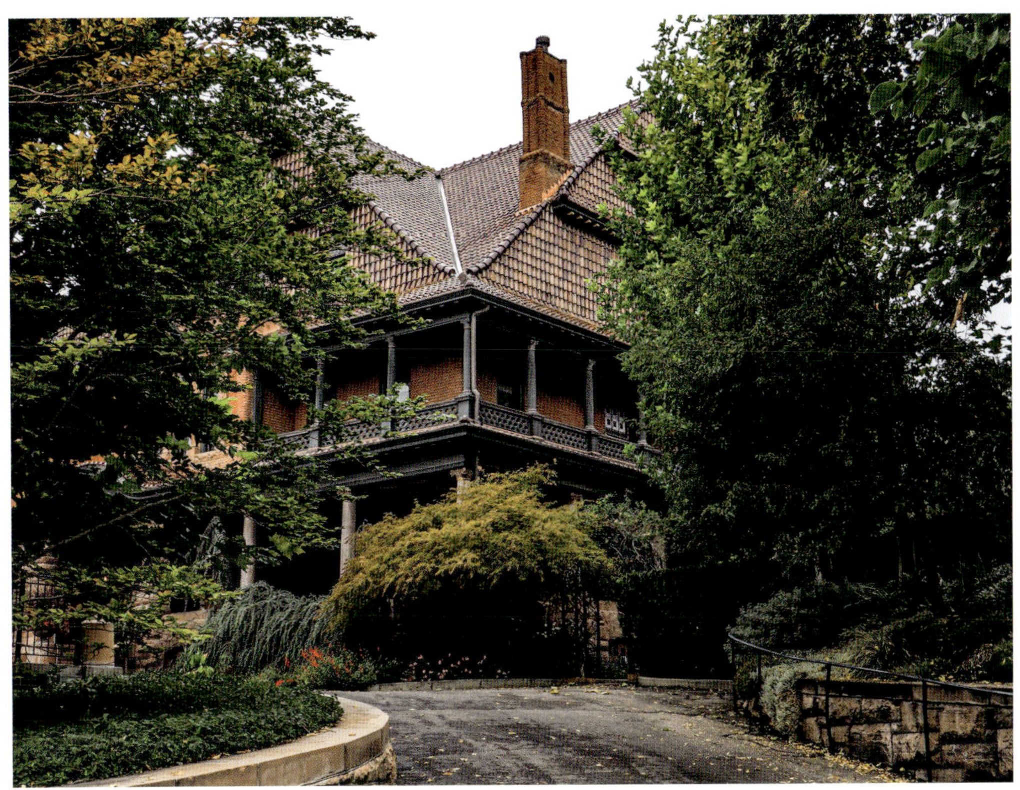

One last look.

3

Masonic Lodge

The Salt Lake City Freemason Lodge was devised in 1920 by several local Freemasons. Their current lodge was at capacity, so a new larger lodge was needed. Completed in 1927, the Egyptian Revival architectural style stands out among the old homes near downtown. Containing lounges, auditoriums, offices, ballrooms, four lodge rooms, and several large and small halls, the impressive structure fills the brain with wonder about what lies behind its walls.

The grand Egyptian architecture drew me in from the nearby street. Seemingly out of place, the symbols and statues give the feeling of ancient wisdom and knowledge. The Masonic Lodge and its organization have given off the vibe of secrecy since its inception. Tours of the great building were once offered to the public but are no longer allowed today. After reaching out to the Masons themselves, I was informed that tours have stopped, not due to the pandemic, but because of vandalism and theft. Tired of having their great temple robbed of small artifacts, the Masons have officially stopped public tours here in Salt Lake City. For now, we'll just have to admire it from the outside.

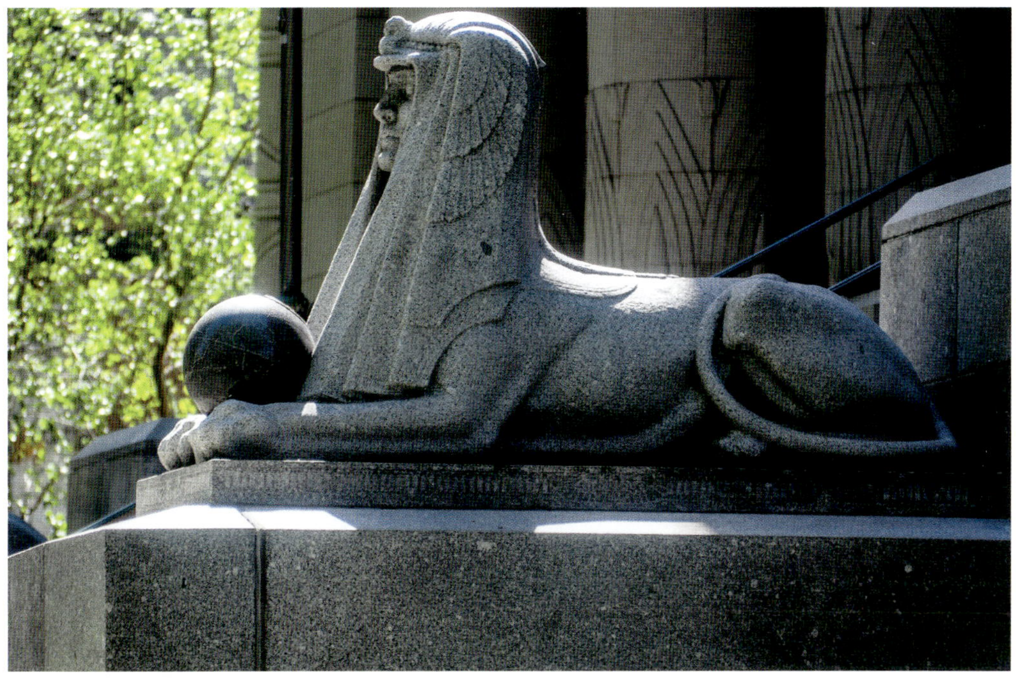

Sitting guard.

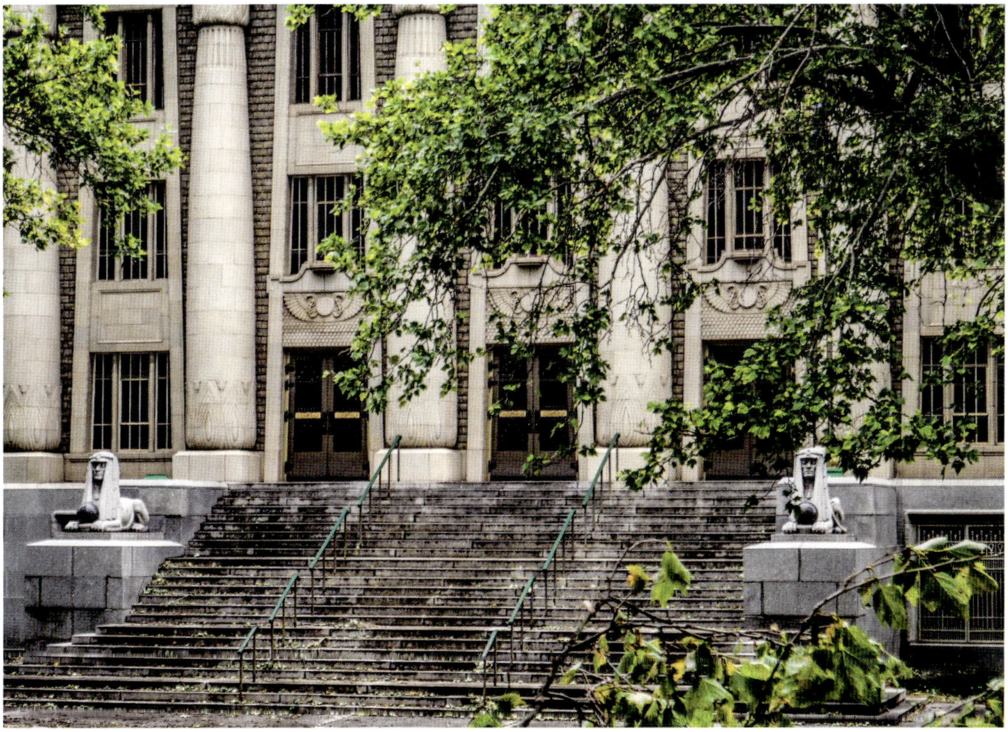

Entrance to the stunning Masonic Temple.

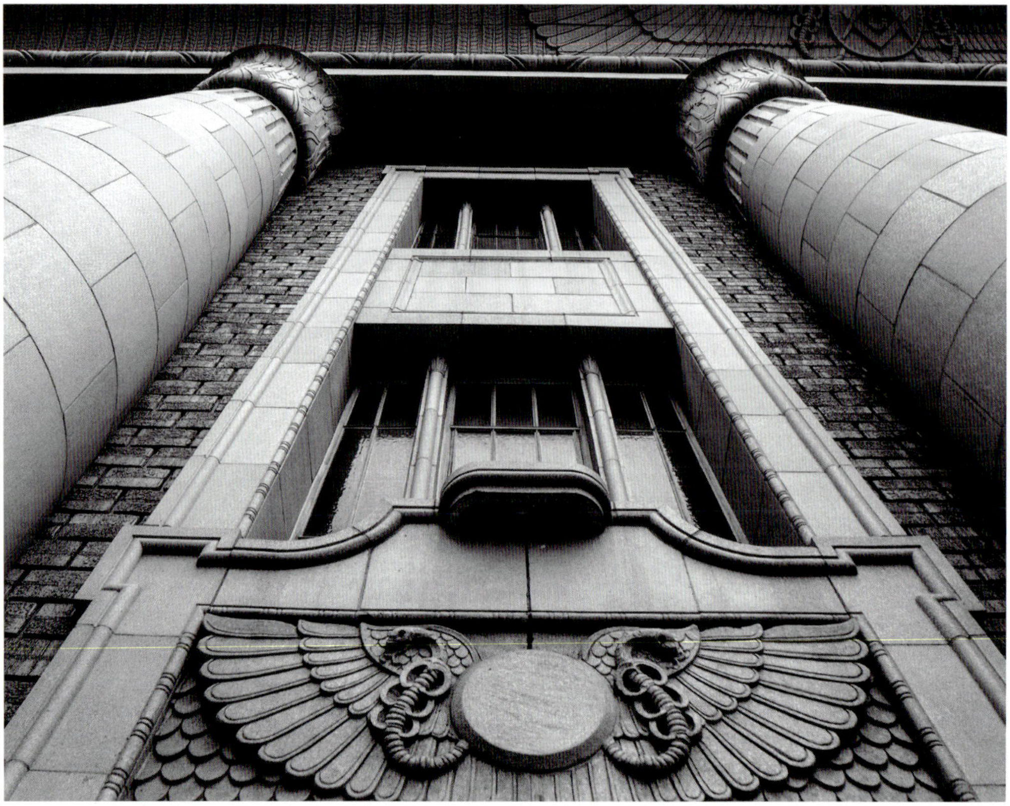

The beautifully designed building represents the order's grand philosophy.

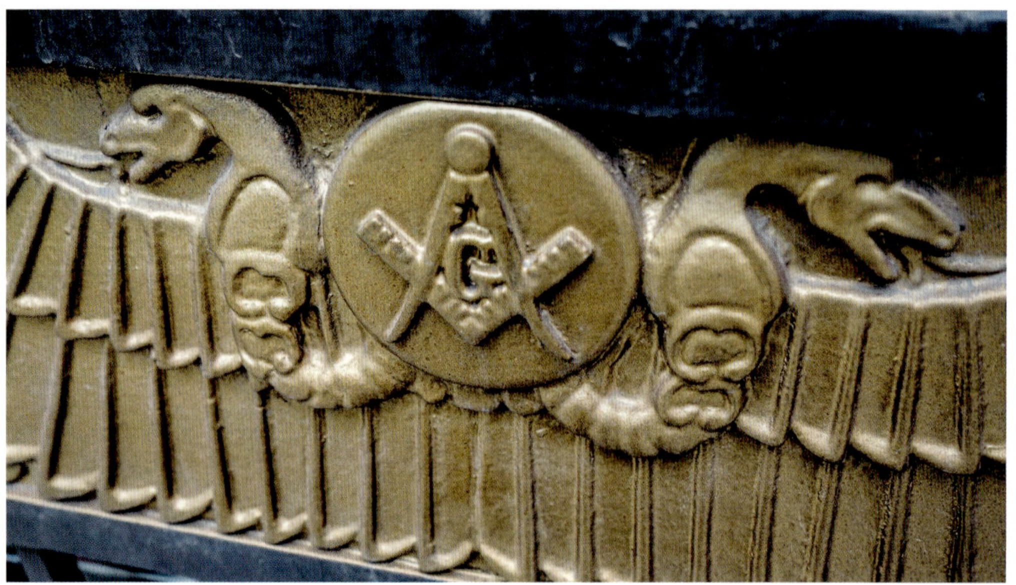

Not-so-hidden symbols were built into the temple.

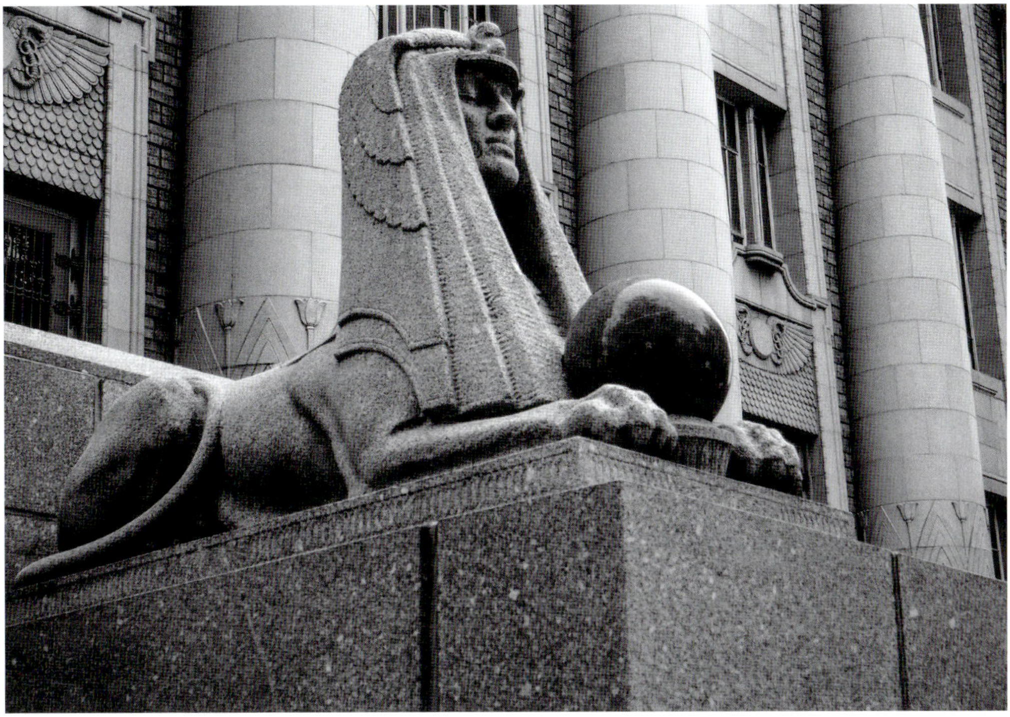

Egyptian theming played a significant role in the design of the temple.

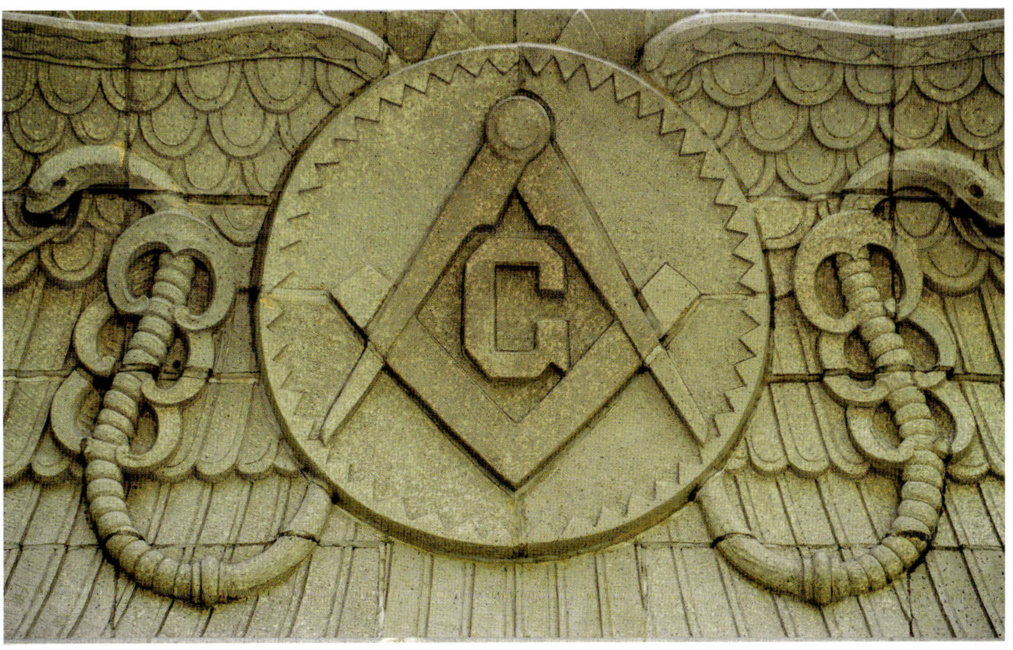

Square and compass.

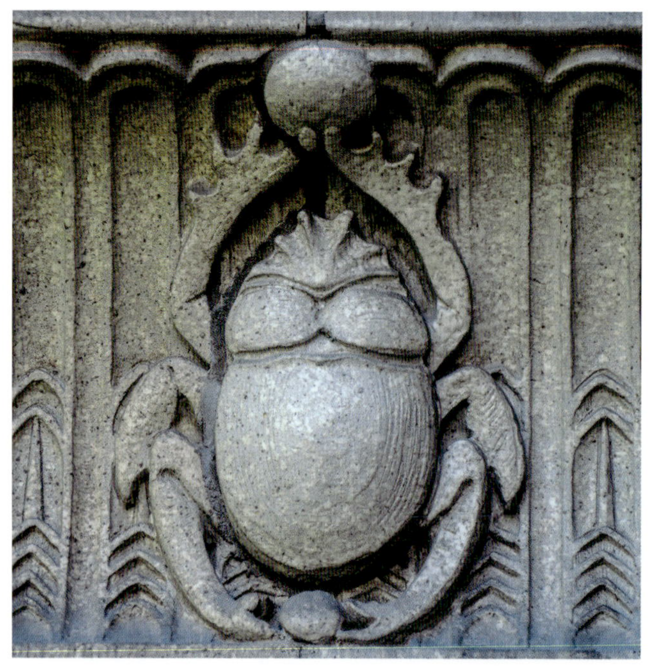

The closer you look, the more symbols you'll find.

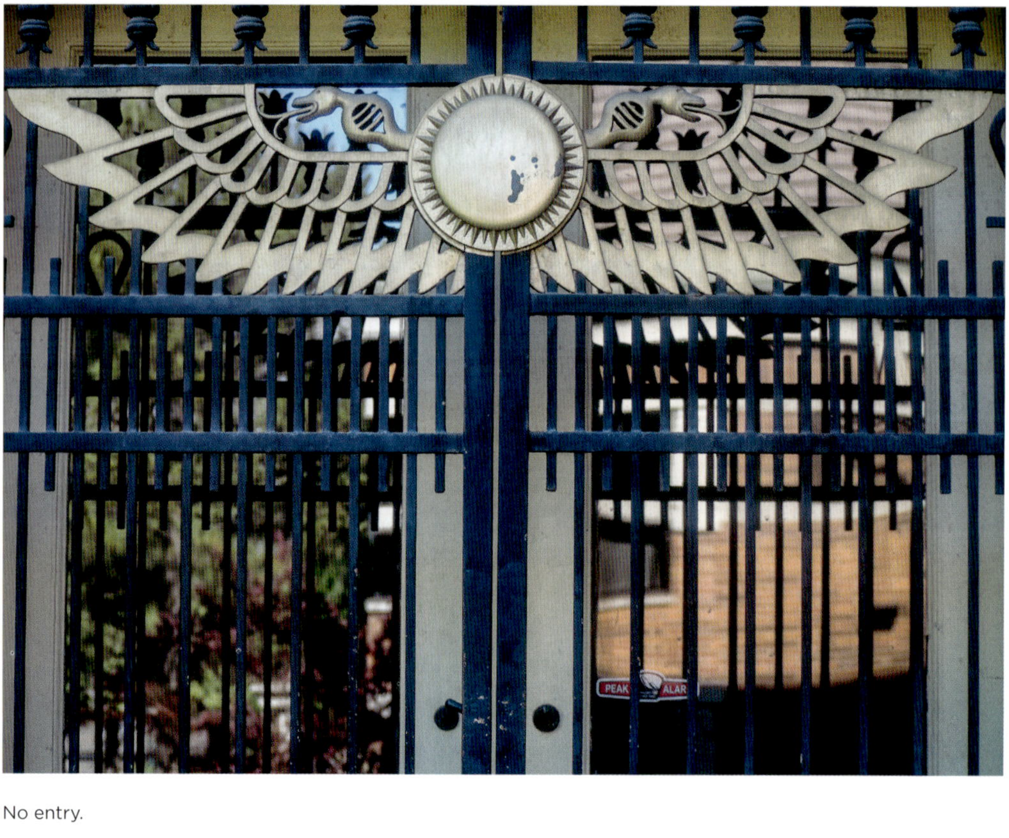

No entry.

4

Gilgal Sculpture Garden

A unique and seemingly hidden gem of Salt Lake City is the Gilgal Sculpture Garden. Tucked away off a quiet street, the entrance often goes unnoticed. Once you near the garden, a pathway lined with trees beckons you to enter. What awaits is a bizarrely spectacular series of sculptures that represent the beliefs of the artist.

Thomas Battersby Child Jr. began work on his then backyard sculpture garden in 1945. Being a professional mason and contractor by trade, Thomas worked on his garden in his free time. He wanted his garden to become a refuge for visitors, offering a peaceful location surrounded by inspiring art. Being religiously minded, the majority of his sculptures reflect his beliefs. But Gilgal is open to everyone. Thomas did not intend to push his ideas onto visitors. His ultimate goal was to harbor creativity. By offering such a unique park, he encouraged visitors to explore the garden and ultimately explore their inner thoughts. He continued to work on his garden up until his death in 1963.

The name, Gilgal, has a biblical origin meaning circle of stones. It is also in the *Book of Mormon*, referring to a specific location. Today the garden is open to the public. It is free to explore and although small, it is well worth a visit.

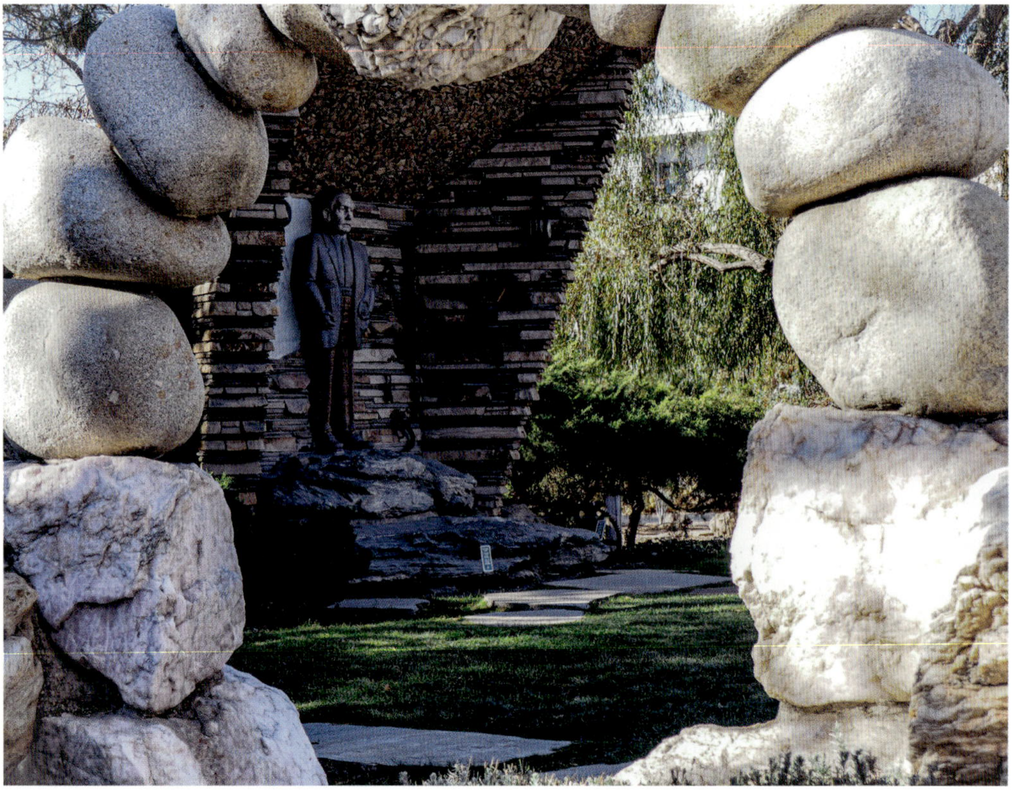

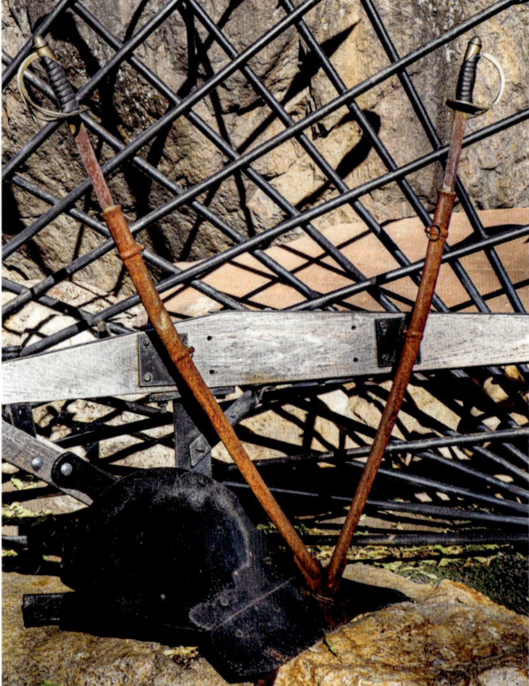

Above: Framed by earth.

Left: Each sculpture can be interpreted in many ways, allowing the viewer to ponder their beliefs.

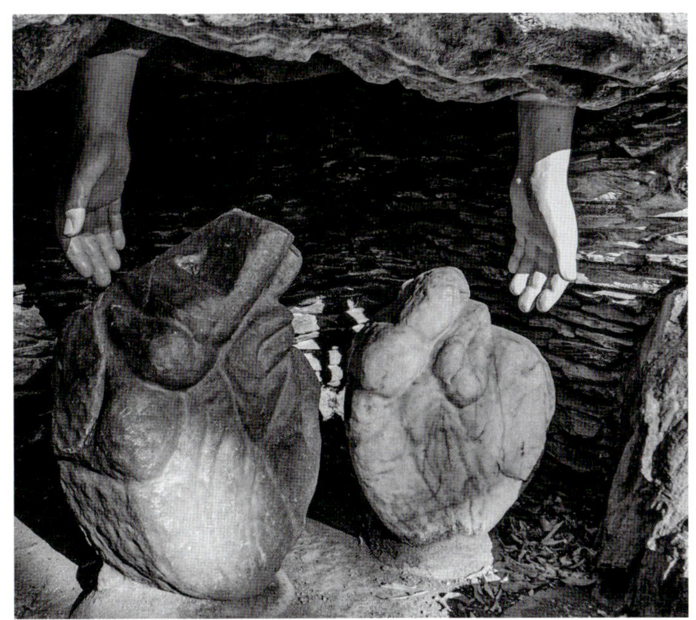

Hearts and hands.

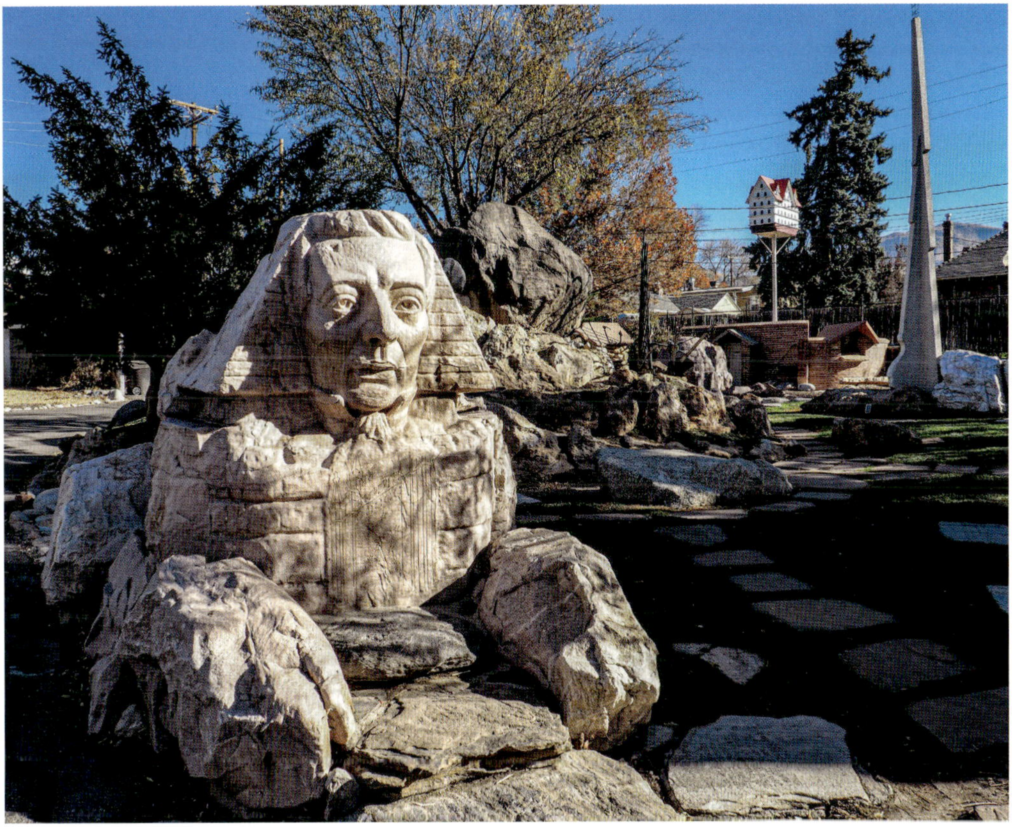

Watching over the garden.

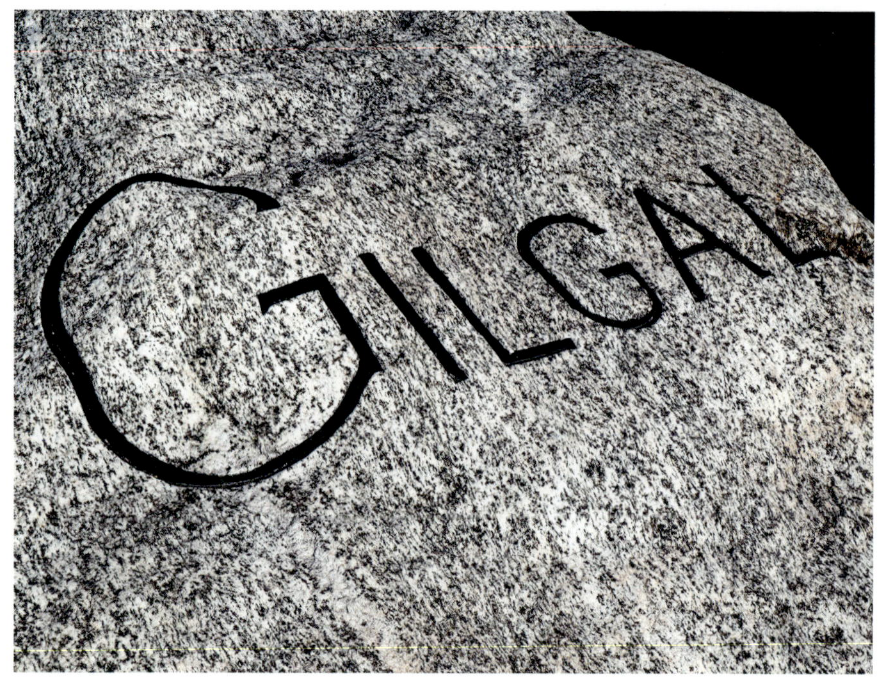

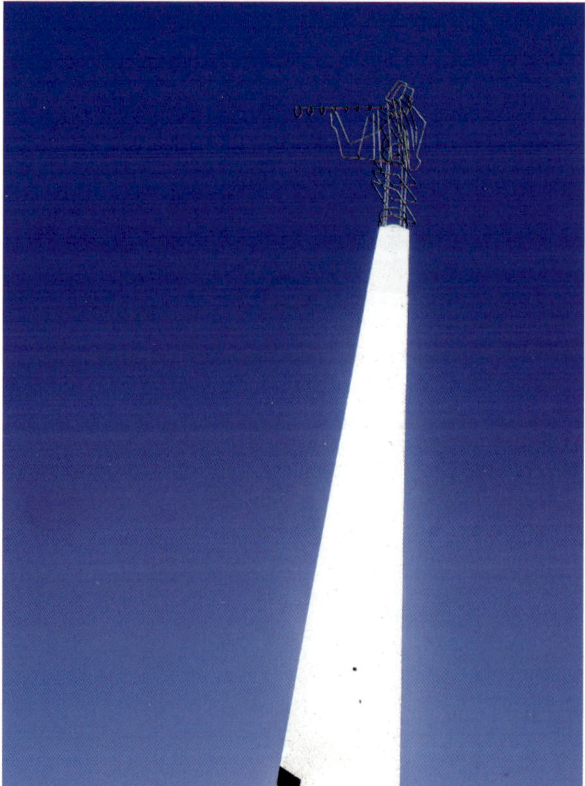

Above: Carved in stone.

Left: Sounding the horns to heaven.

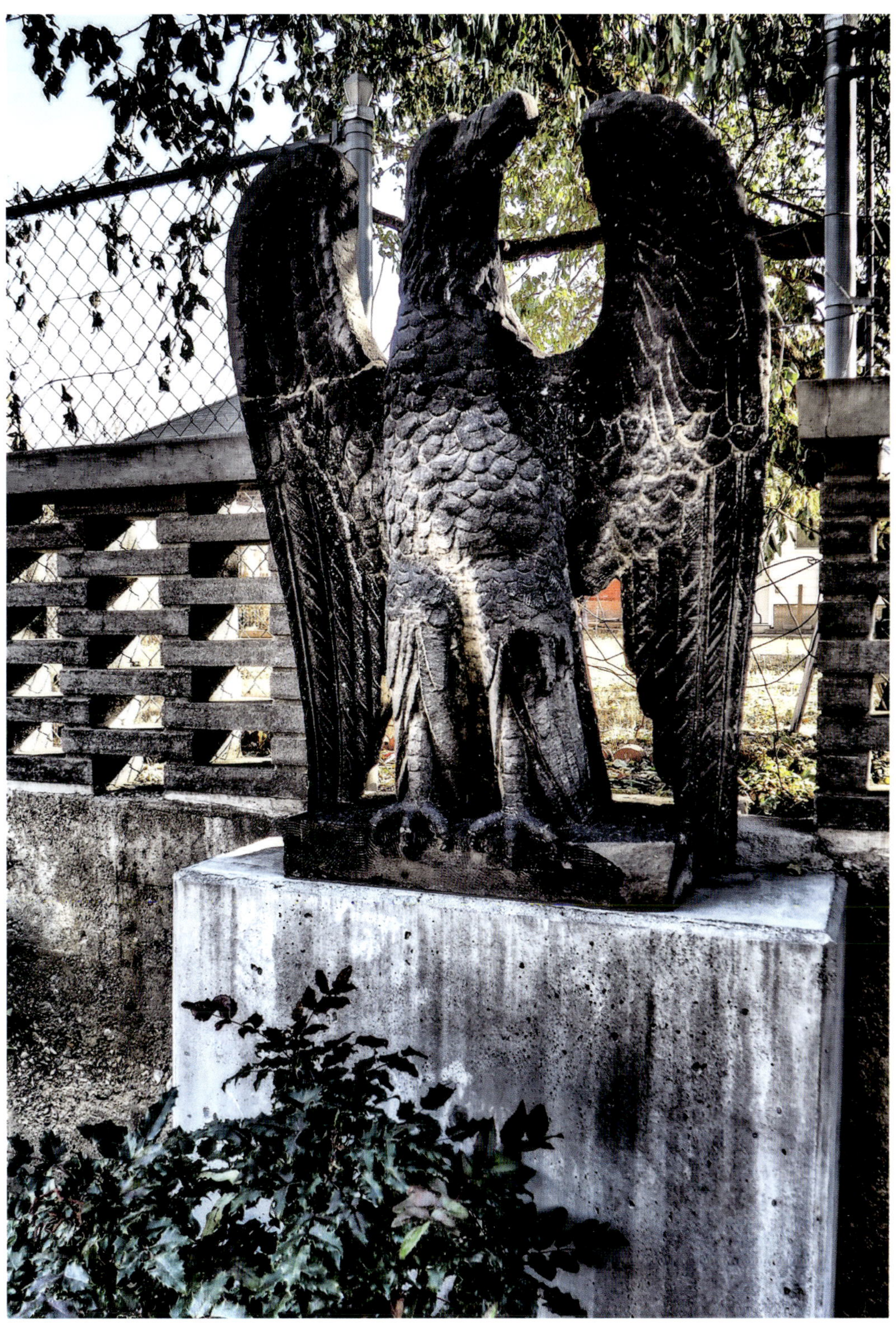

Standing guard.

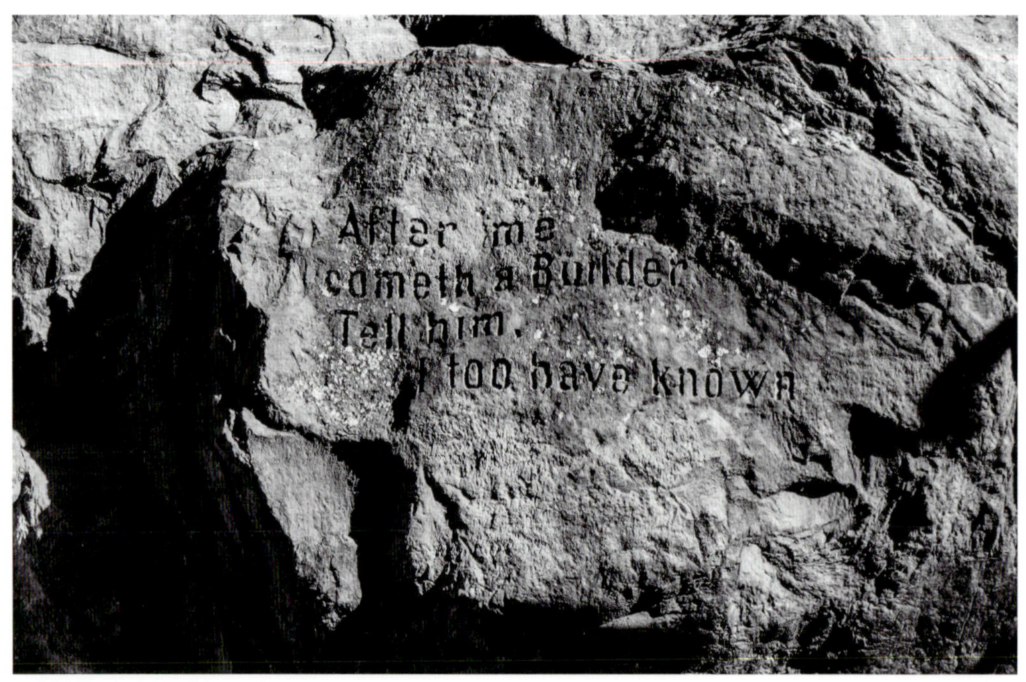

"After me cometh a Builder."

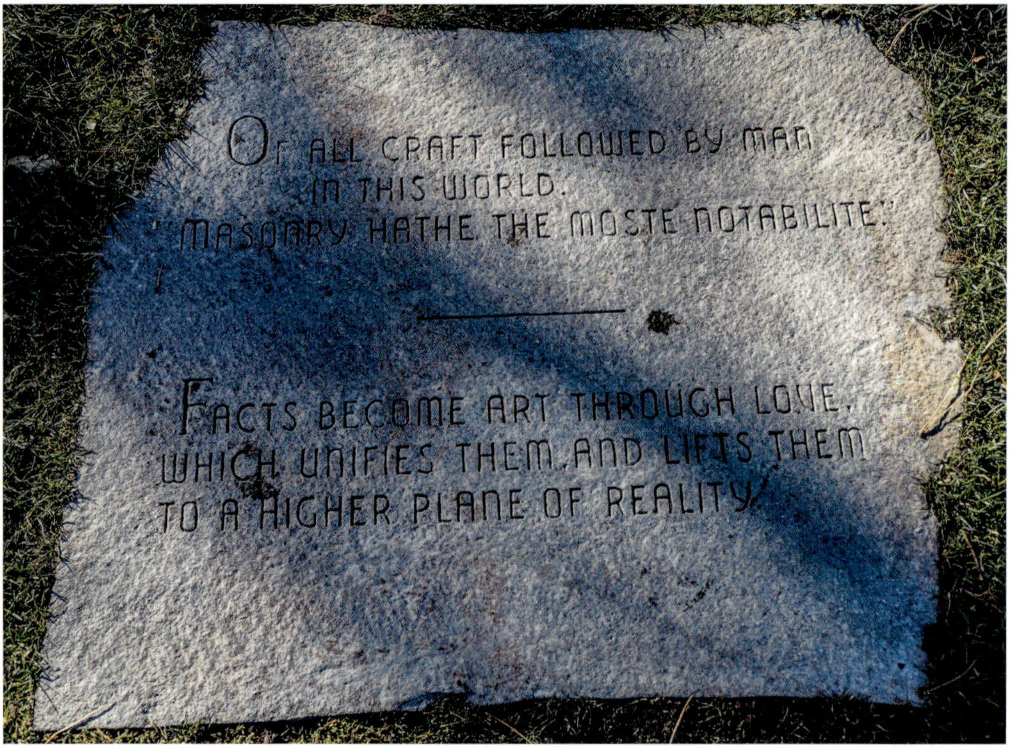

Quotes and passages hide throughout the garden.

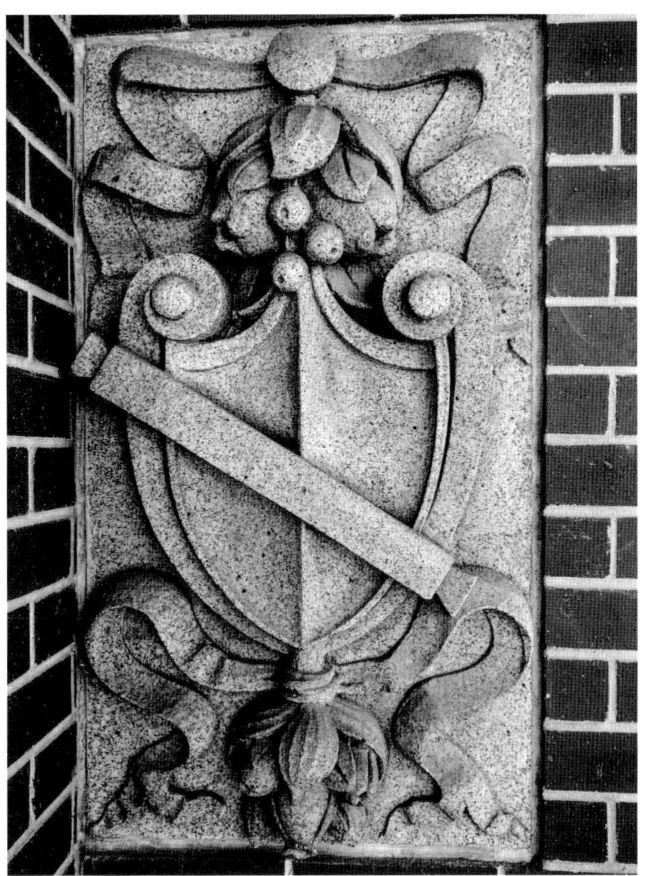

Coat of arms.

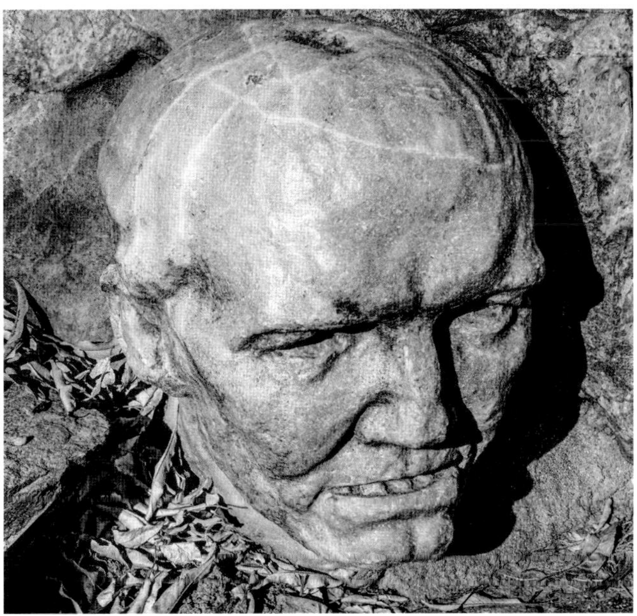

Hardhead.

5

Peace Gardens

Yet another unique garden lies just along the banks of the Jordan River in Salt Lake City. Created by Mrs. Otto Wiesley in 1939, the garden shows peace and unity among all nations. Wiesley worked directly with the mayor, the superintendent of parks, and the Salt Lake Council of Women to achieve her goal. The dedication ceremony and opening were planned to take place in 1947. It was ultimately delayed due to World War II. It finally opened its gates to the public in 1952.

These days the gardens remain within the care of the Salt Lake Council of Women. Although still in relatively good shape, the council is seeking to restore certain areas of the garden. They have asked the public to submit old photos to their website to help with the restoration process. Please submit if you have any photos! There are twenty-six nations currently represented throughout the garden. Each nation has its own section containing statues of peace leaders, architectural pieces, and native vegetation specific to that nation.

True to its namesake, the gardens offer beautiful areas that will be sure to bring you peace and tranquility. Free to the public, all are encouraged to wander amongst the nations. We could all use a reprieve from our chaotic world. The Peace Gardens offer a glimpse into an ideal world of unity, a world where peace and kindness reign supreme.

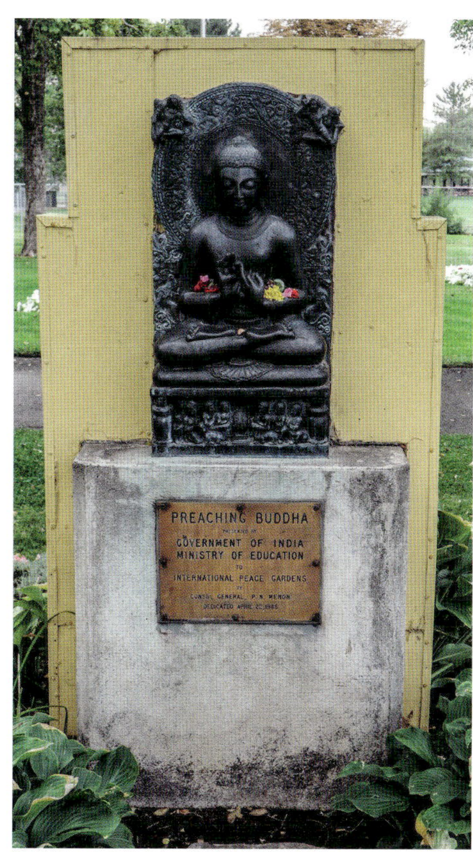

Right: Preaching Buddha.

Below: Mahatma.

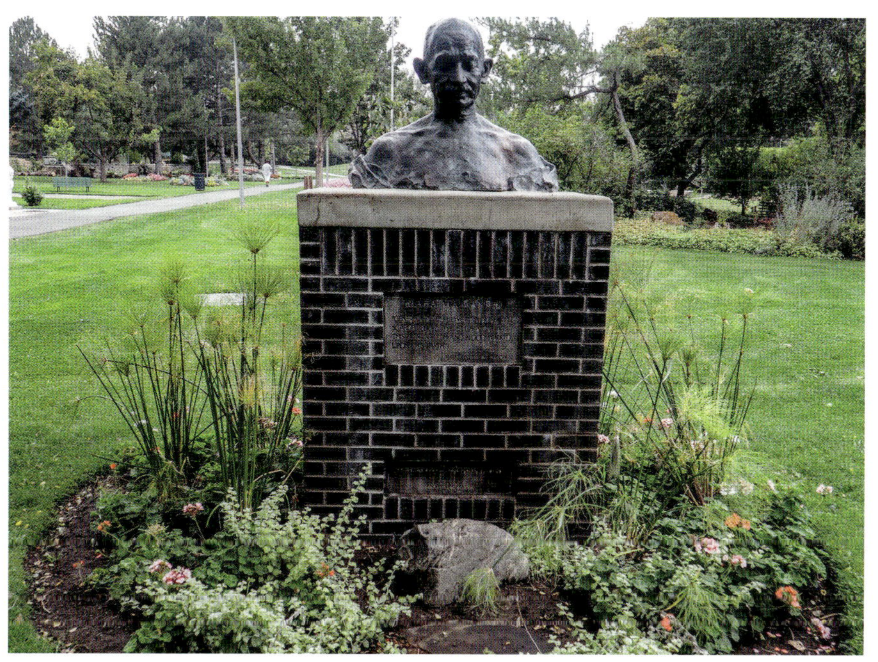

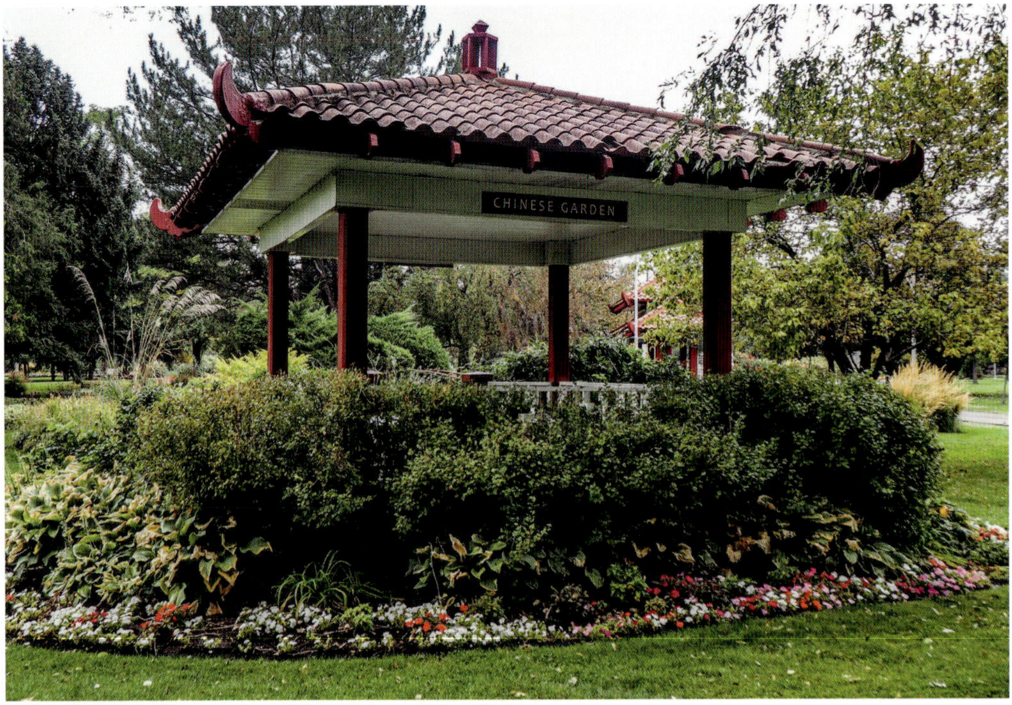

The Chinese Gardens are a beautiful section of the park showcasing their countries classic architecture.

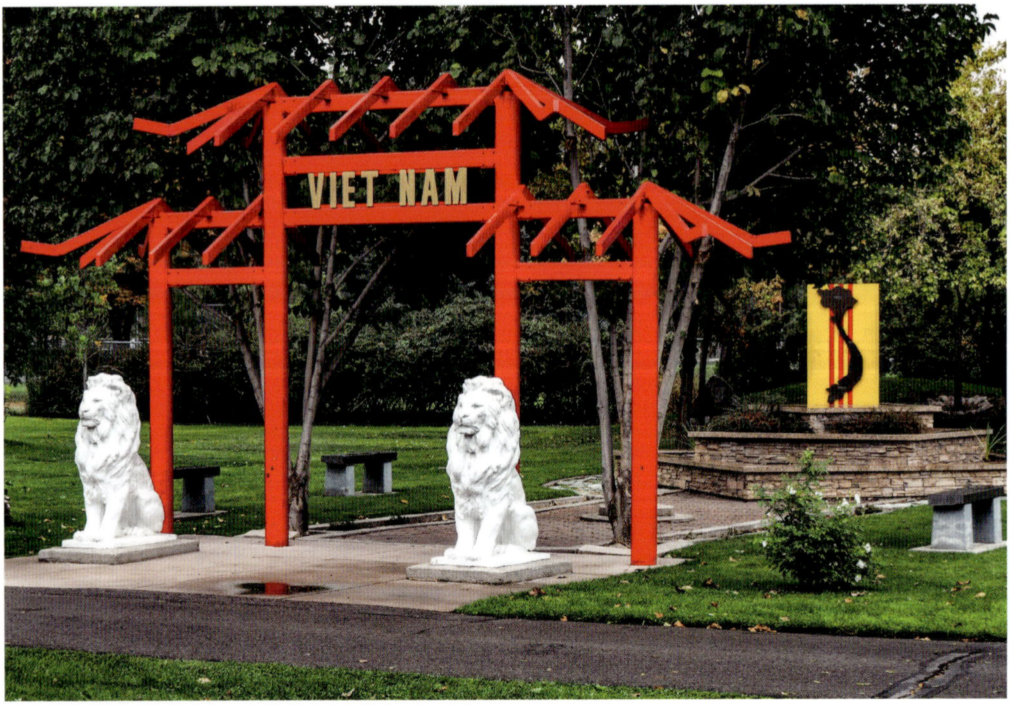

Lions guard the entrance to Vietnam.

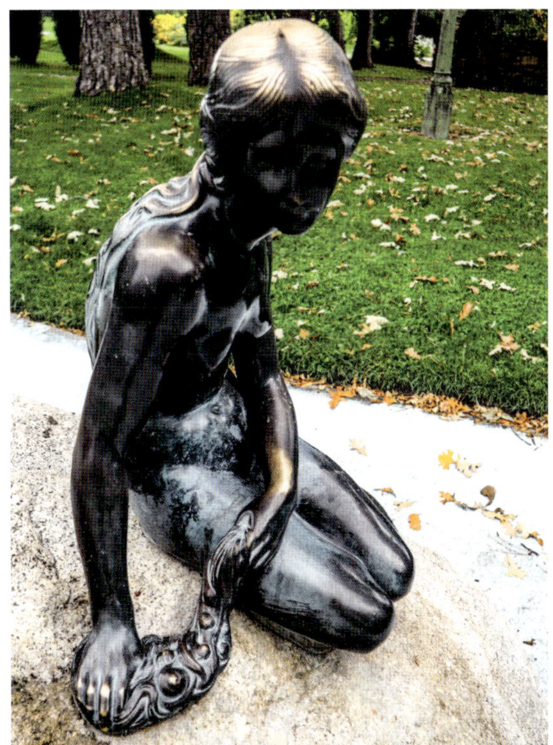

Right: Mermaid maiden.

Below: Head down the path, for you never know what you'll find.

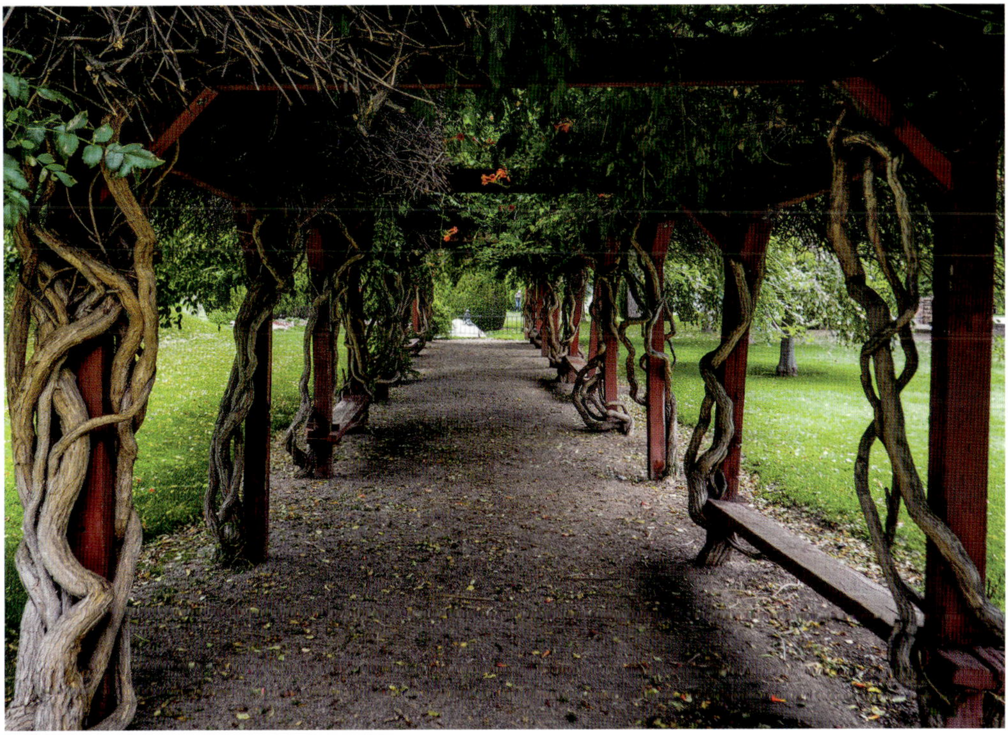

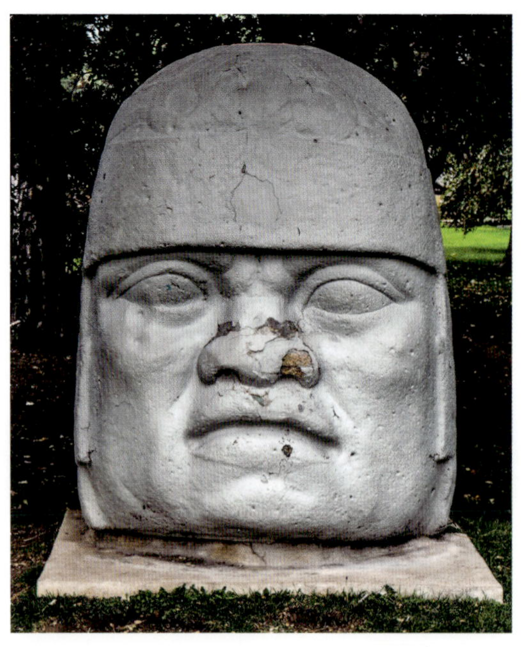

You'll lose this staring contest.

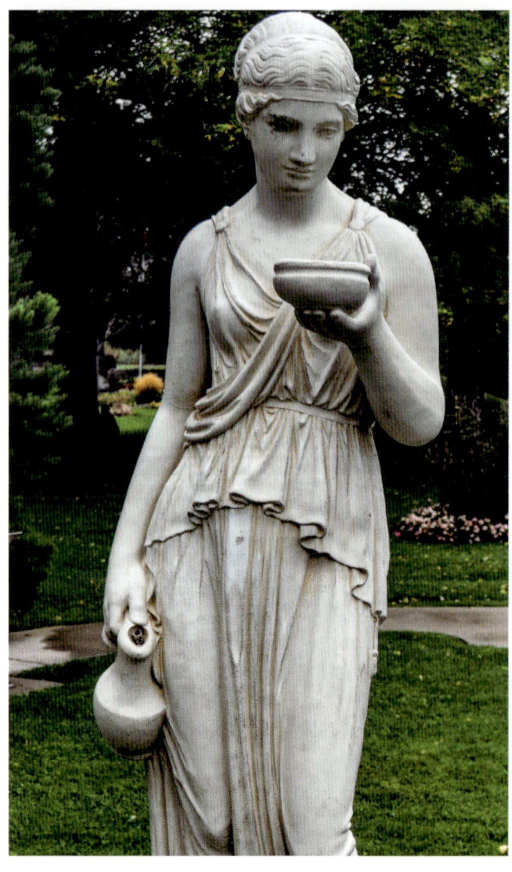

Beauty in stone.

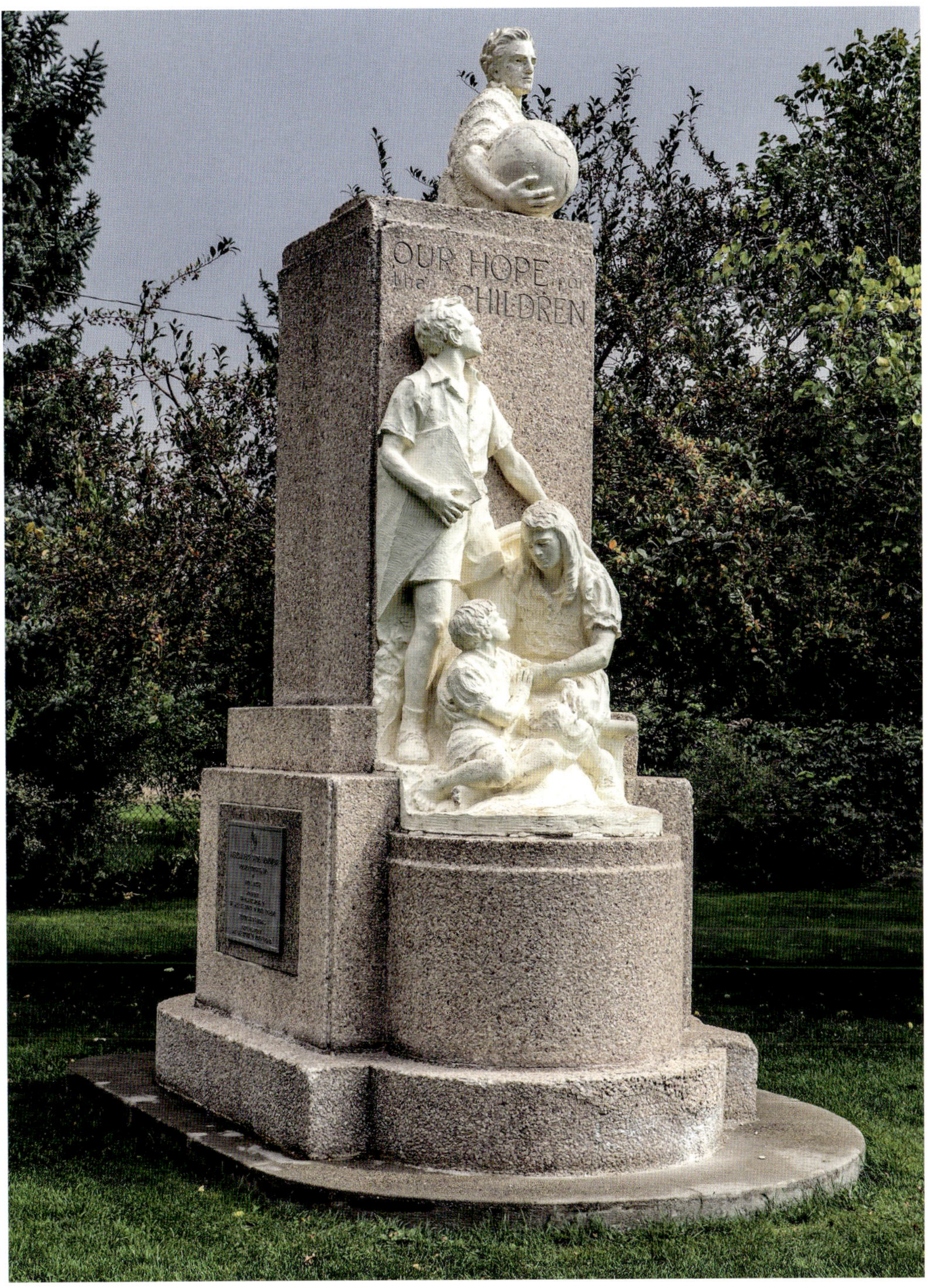

Our hope.

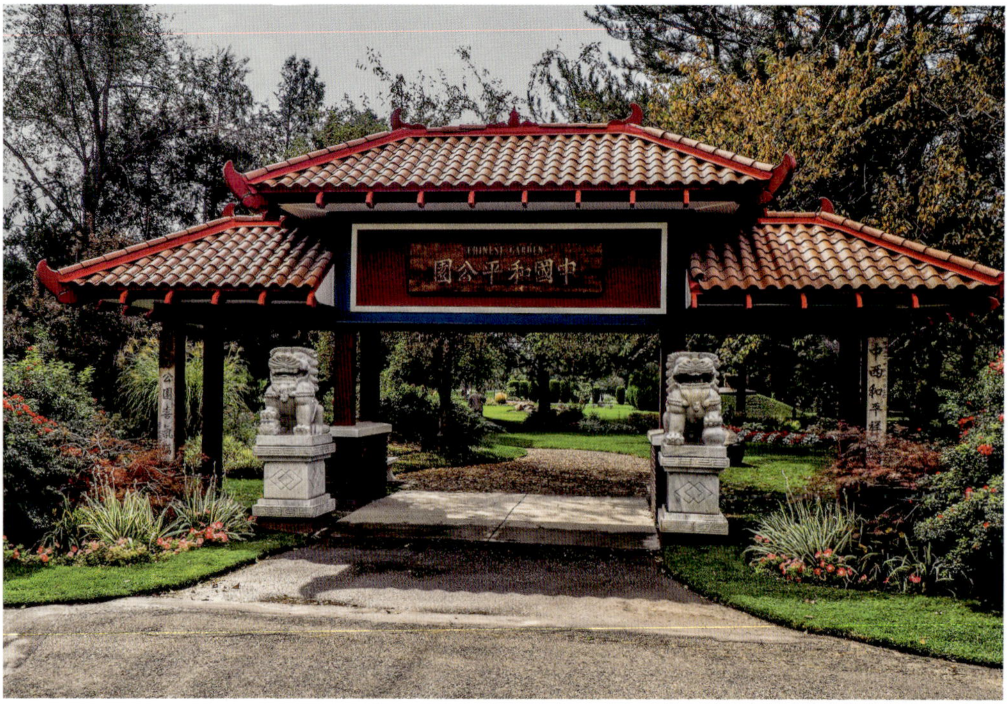

Welcome to the Chinese Garden.

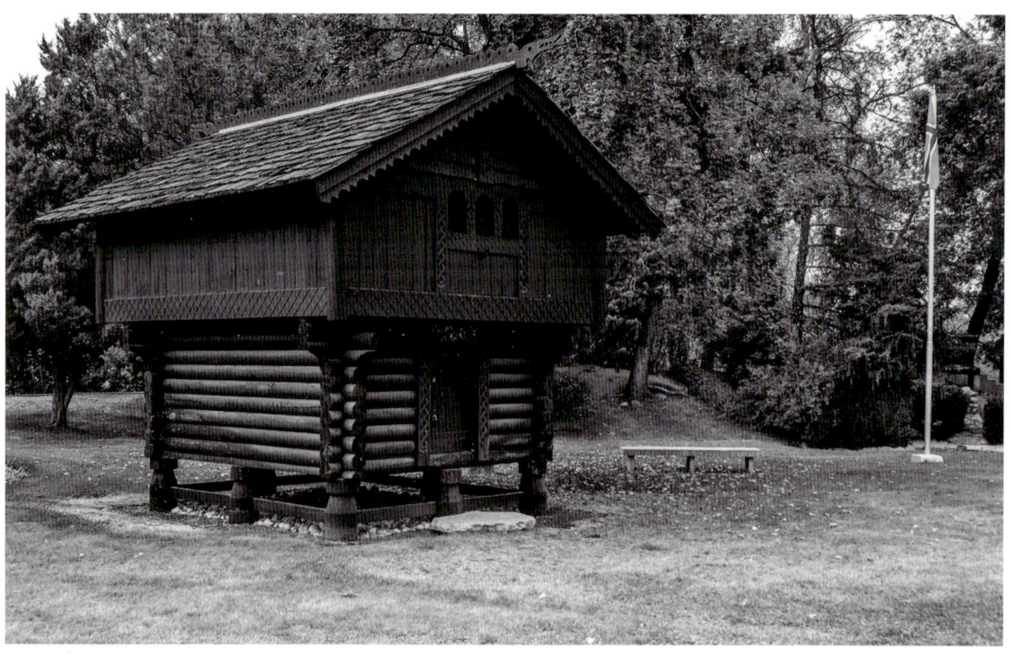

Take a stroll through multiple countries.

6

Fisher Mansion

Built in 1893, the Fisher Mansion was constructed along a small section of the Jordan River. Fisher chose this location because of the water source that he needed to supply his brewery. Having immigrated from Germany in 1881, he would soon become a highly successful brewer. By 1905, his company had become one of the largest breweries in the west, employing fifty people and producing roughly 75,000 barrels of brew. Fisher owned many taverns throughout the Salt Lake Valley, creating a constant demand for his creation.

Fisher was at constant odds with the dominant local religion. Beer drinkers were seen as immoral degenerates in the eyes of the Mormon Church. To combat these prevailing views, Fisher created pro-beer ads. The ads were a huge success, and business was booming, but the boom would not last. Fisher was forced to cease production in 1918. Prohibition would cause its early demise.

Fisher wouldn't live to see the brewery re-open. He died of kidney failure near the time of its closure. His son continued brewing and he re-opened in 1933. Being the only brewery to survive prohibition, Fishers Brewing would thrive for several years. After two decades, Fisher's son sold the brewery in 1955 to a San Francisco company named Lucky Lager. While the business and brewery have long since been gone, the mansion stands the test of time.

For roughly fifty years, the mansion stayed within the Fisher family. Eventually, it was leased to the Catholic Church in 1945. The church used it as a convent until 1970 when it became an all-male drug and alcohol treatment facility. The mansion housed forty-one recovering addicts and even provided them with employment assistance. As the years went by, the estate would become abandoned and fall into decay. Decades without upkeep have given the mansion its haunting look. Plans have been in the works to restore and re-purpose the mansion. In 2006, the city bought the property with hopes of one day restoring it to its original beauty. As of now, not much work has been done, and the property still sits more or less abandoned.

I initially had never heard about the Fisher Mansion, but rather spotted it early one morning on my way to the airport. From the highway, it looked like a boarded-up mansion right out of a horror film. Later, I found my way to the mansion and commenced my exploration. Remnants of a grand garden surround the property. Overgrown rose bushes and vines snake their way around the front yard. Nestled beside the Jordan River, the location would be perfect if not for nearby homeless encampments. I highly discourage visiting this area at night or alone.

While unable to enter the mansion, it is easily viewed and photographed from a nearby paved trail. A historical information sign briefly describes the history of the Fisher Mansion. It's an epic area to visit. Ornate masonry lines the exterior adding to the mansions opulent design. Its beautiful decay makes it one of my favorite local mansions to see. Boarded-up windows add to the creepy atmosphere. It's easy to imagine ghosts wandering its halls, or a witch stirring her cauldron in the basement.

With preservation efforts in the works, my dream is to one day explore and photograph the stunning interior. Either way, it is well worth a visit.

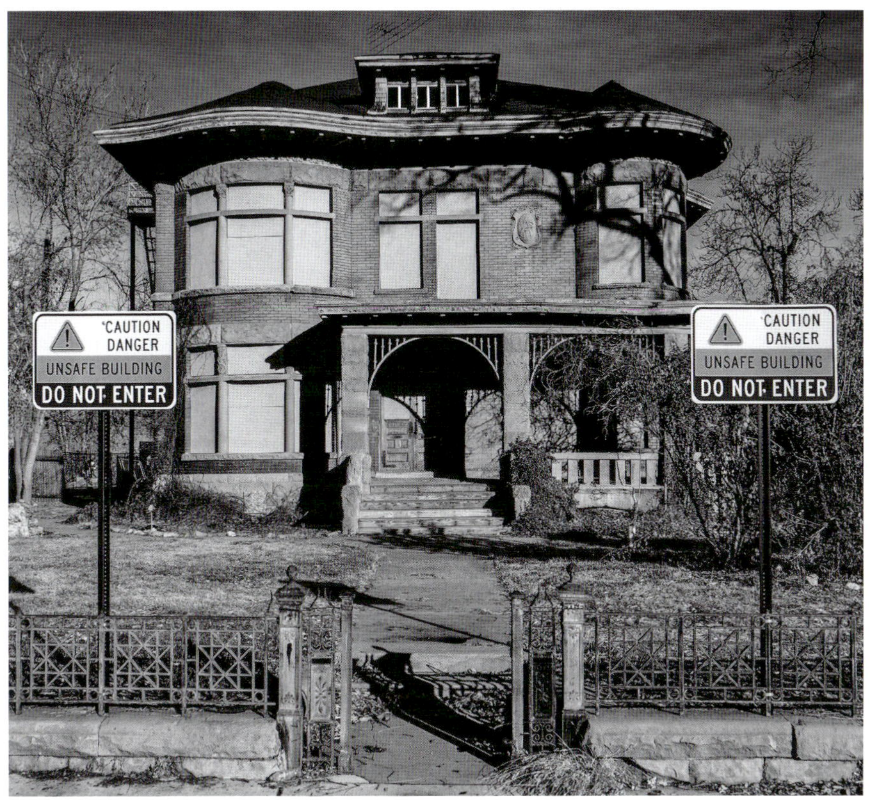

Danger attracts.

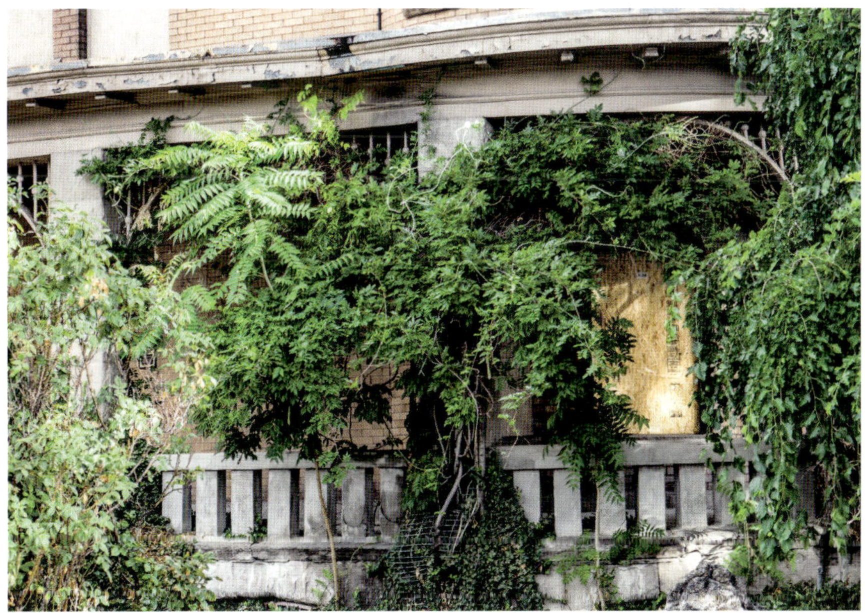

Nature slowly reclaims.

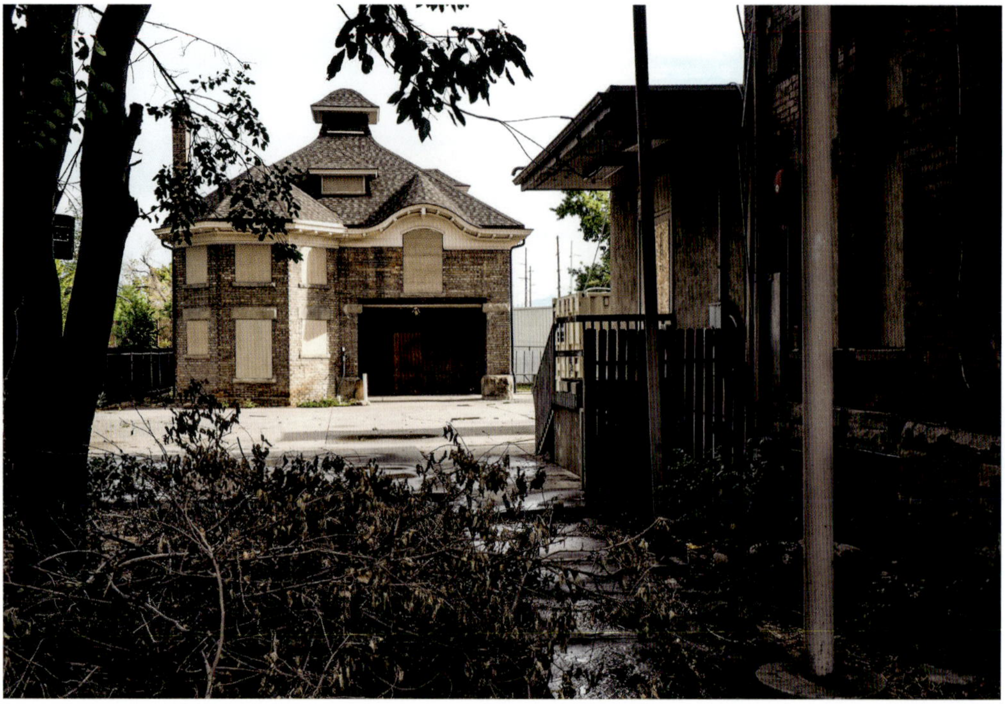

Looking towards the Carriage House.

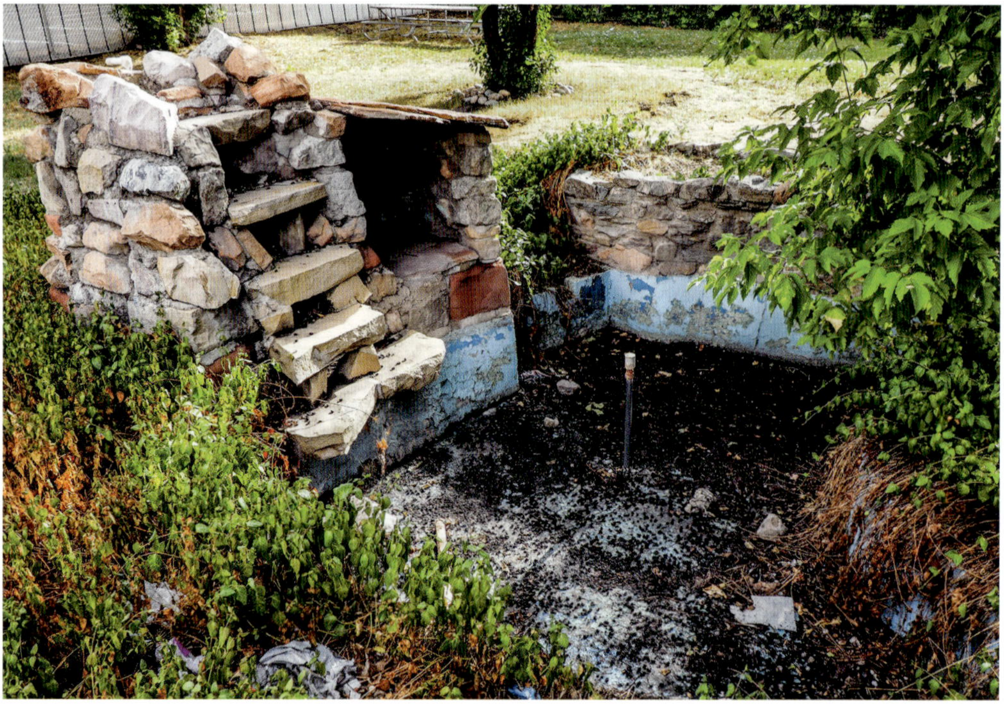

An old fountain in the once-grand garden.

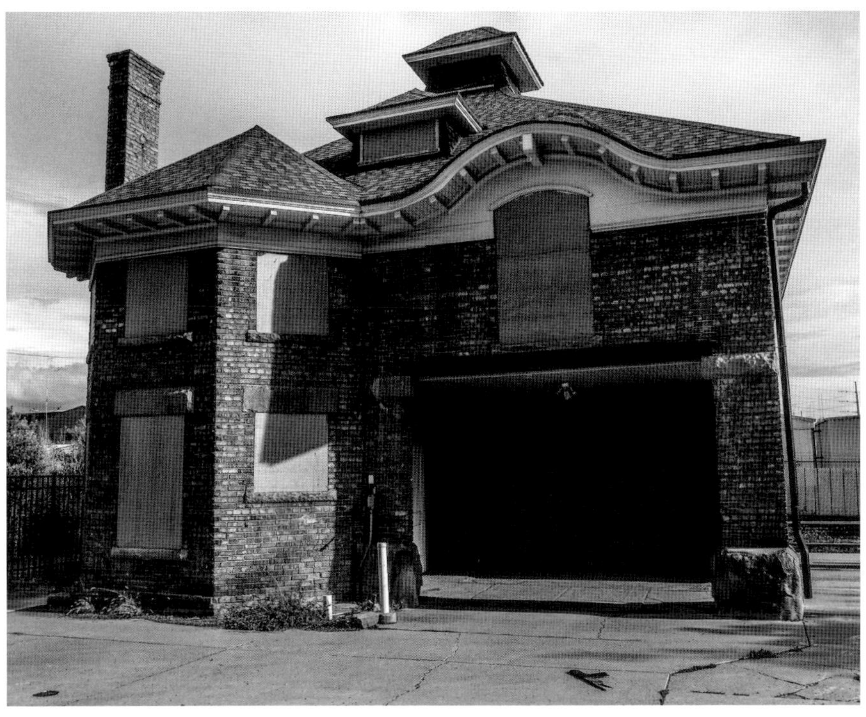

Carriage house.

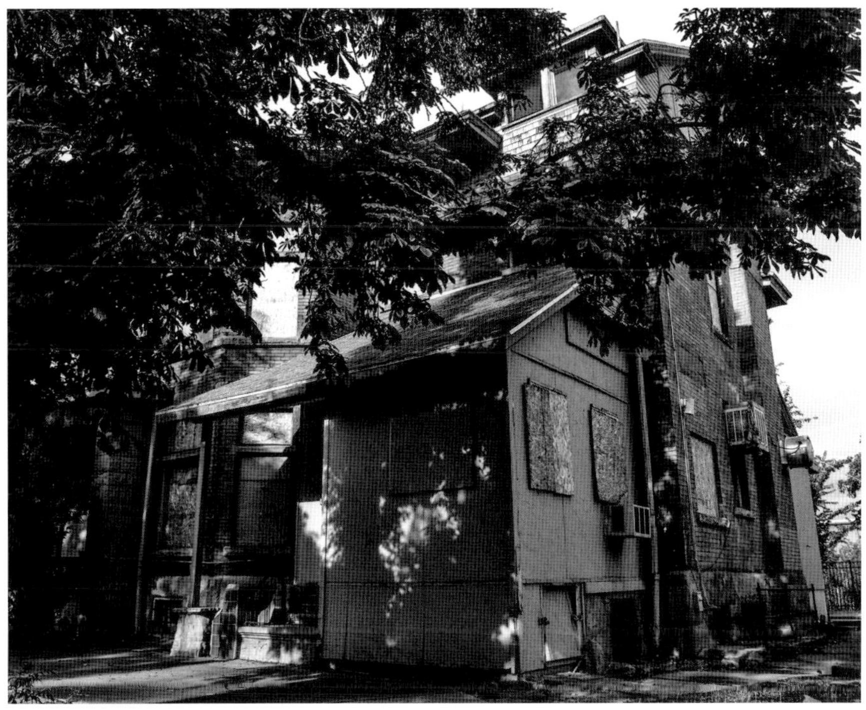

Boards cover every window and door.

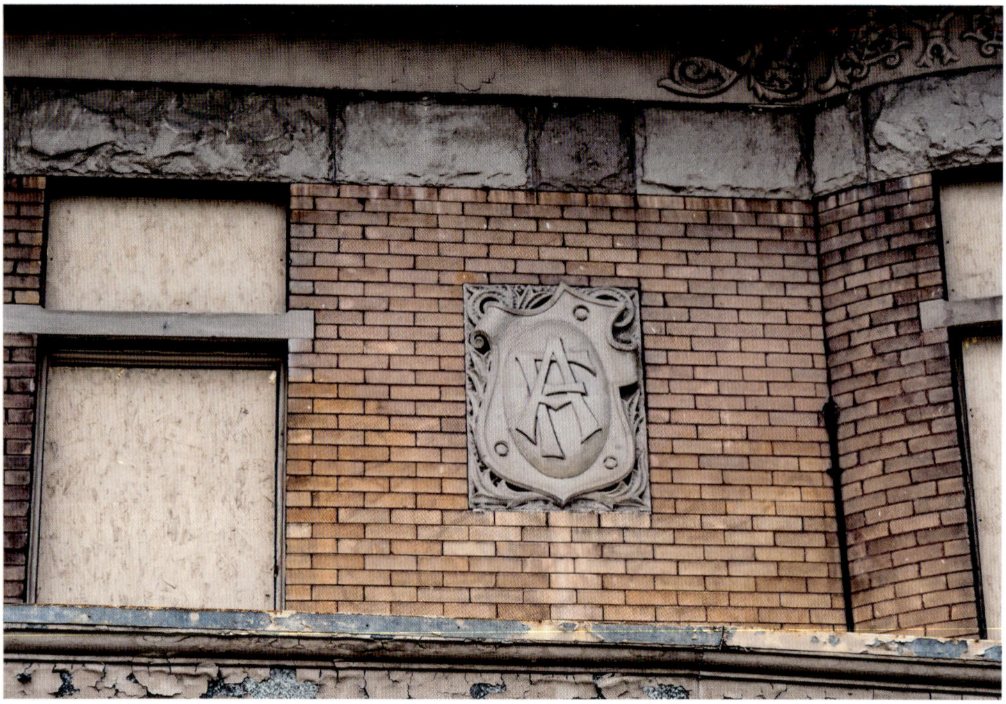

Alfred Fisher.

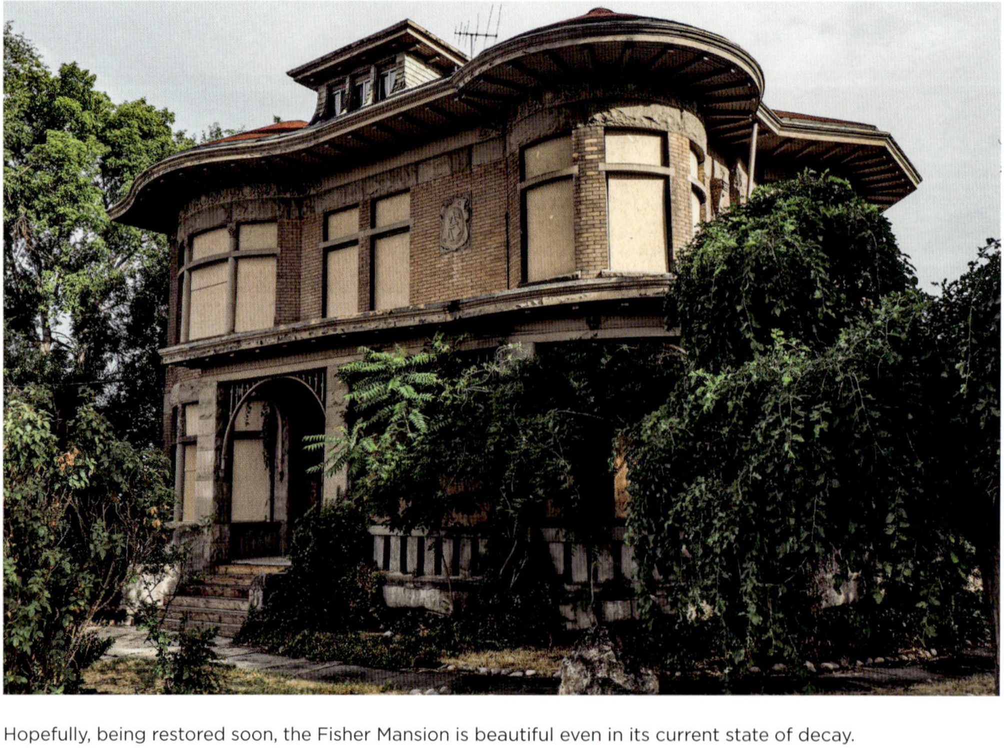

Hopefully, being restored soon, the Fisher Mansion is beautiful even in its current state of decay.

7

Alta Club

Maybe someday I'll become a member of the Alta Club. I can imagine myself sipping a glass of wine while staring out onto the street. I wonder what it would be like to write in the dining room surrounded by the club's dark yet comforting walls. Ah well, until then, I can admire from the streets. Founded in 1883 by wealthy mine industrialists, the club reflects luxury and wealth. This means no entrance for me!

In the beginning, Mormons were banned from entry. The rift died soon as the first Mormon joined just a few years later. Prohibition sparked an internal divide as well. Those in favor were staunchly against any alcohol consumption, while other members were sneaking booze in every chance they could. In the 1930s, the club was struck by the great depression. It struggled to gain members and lost several patrons. Slot machines were installed in an attempt to regain some cash flow. Although controversial at the time, the idea had worked.

Through the years the club has seen its ups and downs. The sheer age of it alone begs the question: is it haunted? Some say most definitely. Way back in the 1950s, a club member lit a cigar and fell asleep. His room caught fire destroying the majority of the third floor. Tragically for him, he was burned to death. Since then he has been spotted lurking on the third floor or sitting on the porch. A ghostly lady of the night has been seen as well. She wanders the halls touching guests with her icy hands. Ghosts or no ghost, the Alta Club is impressive nonetheless.

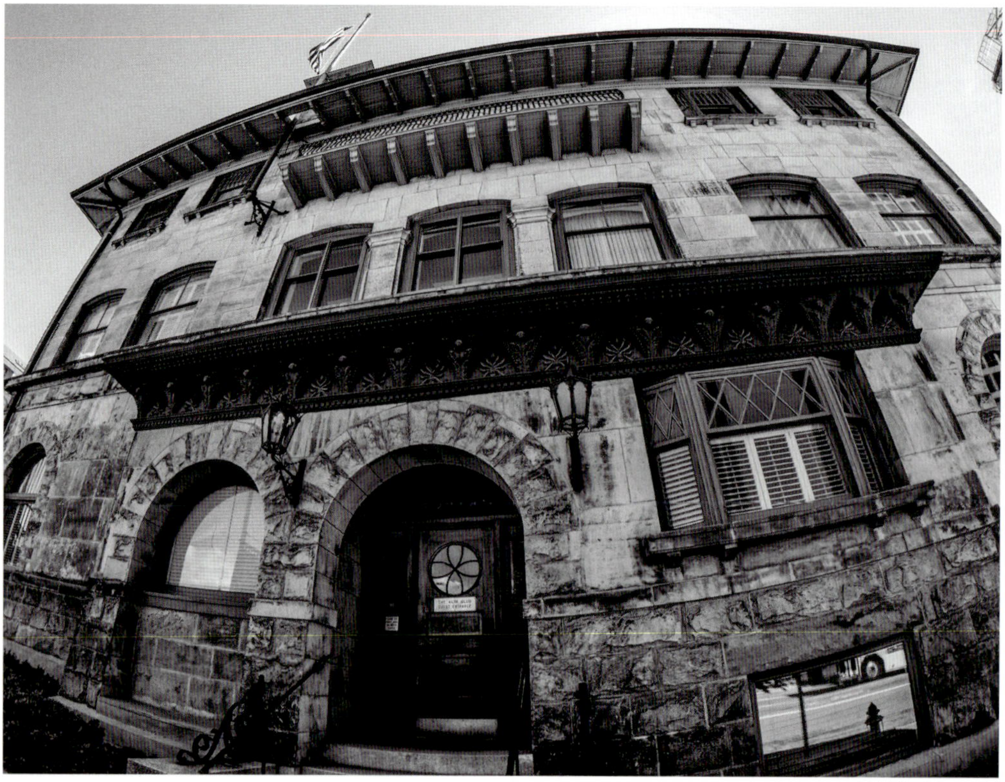

Over 100 years of history dwell within the walls of the Alta Club.

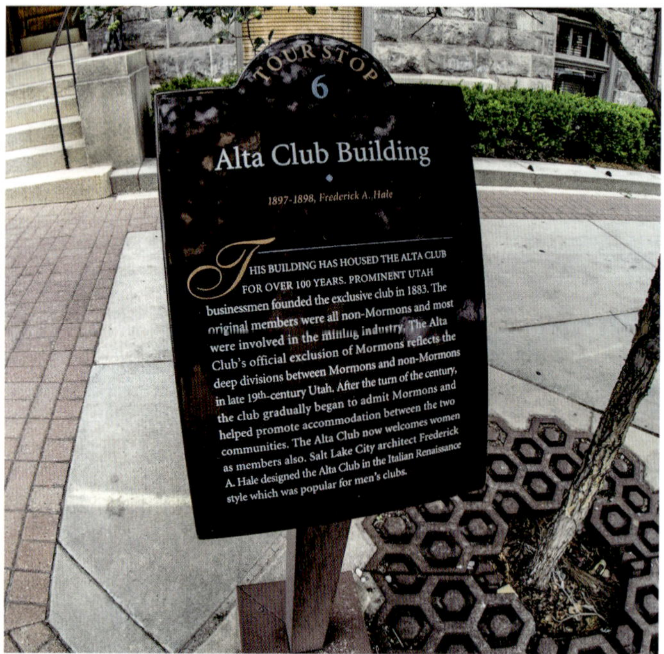

Tour stop.

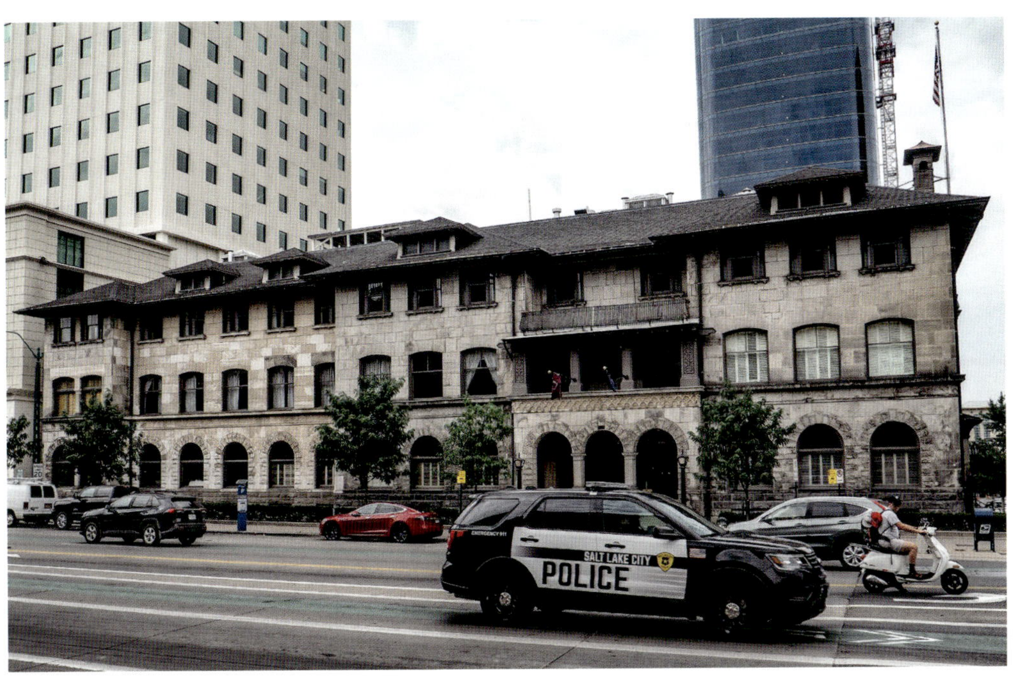

An admirable clash of old and new architecture.

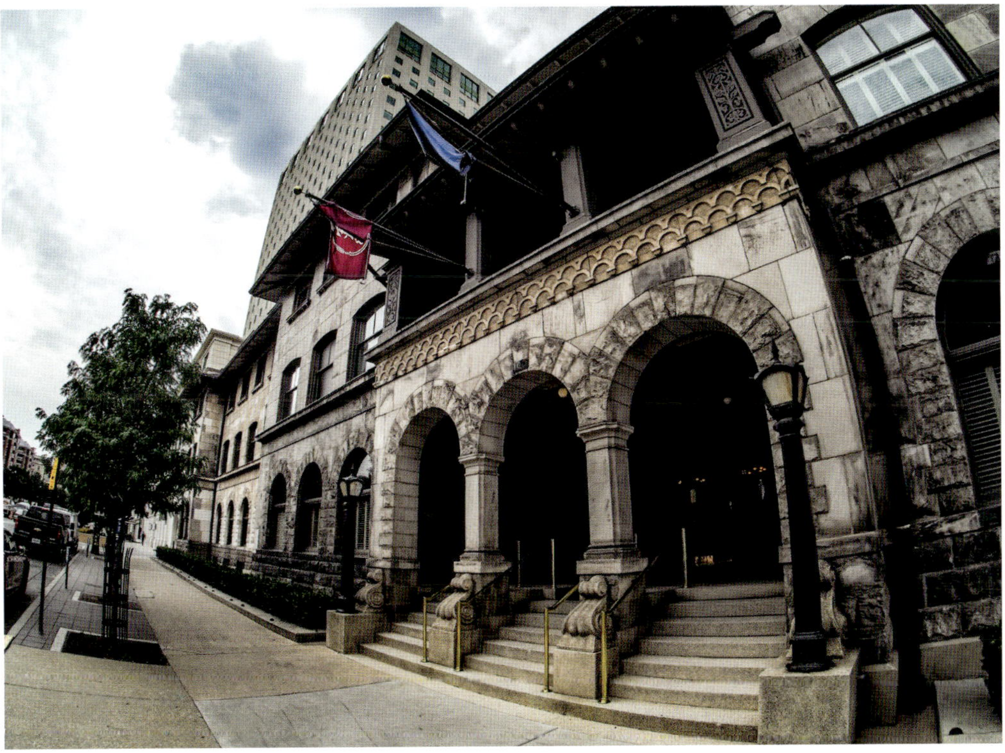

Maybe someday I'll become a member. A man can dream!

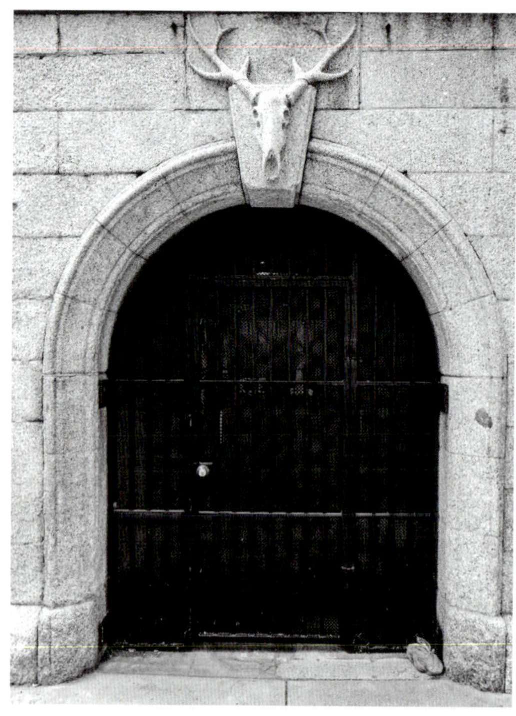

Left: An interesting find nearby.

Below: History is hidden between skyscrapers.

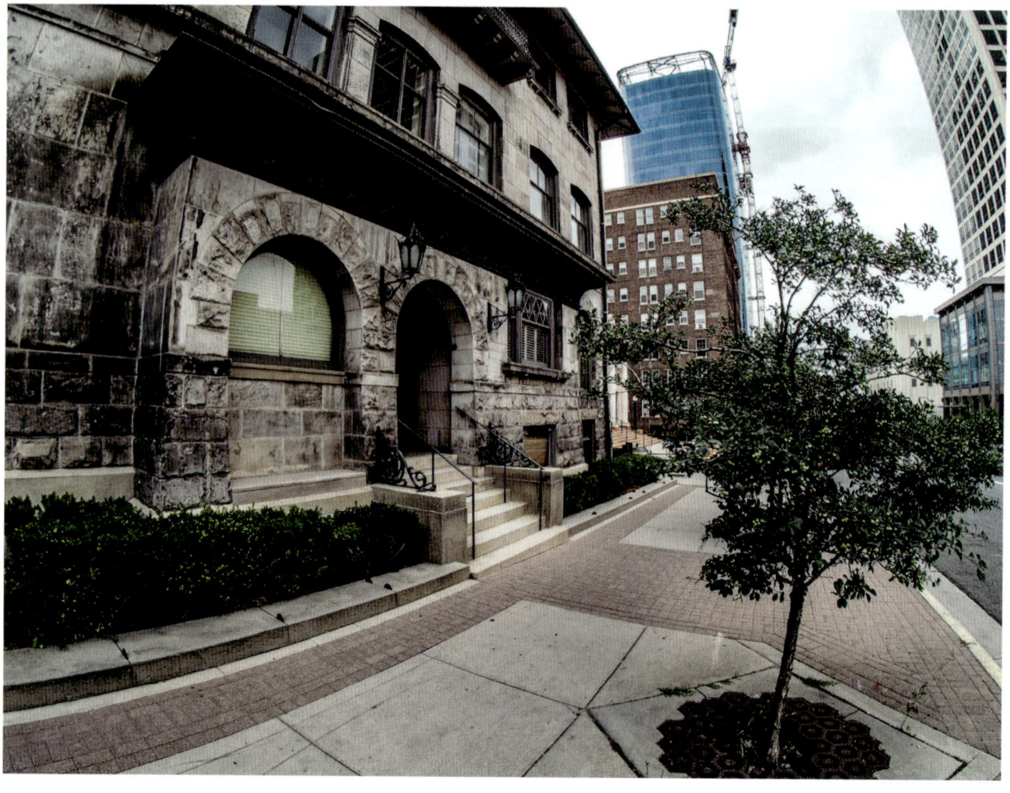

8

Abandoned Waterpark

I couldn't go one book without mentioning abandoned areas. My true passion lies in imaging the dark and dreary. While this book only touches on the abandoned world, you can check out my other book, *Abandoned Utah*. A new book will be released sometime next year via the *Abandoned Union* series. Keep an eye out for it!

While exploring abandoned locations in the Salt Lake area, a different type of threat exists. Yes, the usual danger of collapse and hazards are still present, but an additional threat of drug addicts and homeless squatters lies within these structures. I can't stress this enough: don't go alone, or, if you do, make sure someone knows where you are. Pepper spray and a taser aren't a bad idea either. With that being said, I've never been threatened or felt like I was in danger. What I have encountered is evidence of drug use, theft, and even arson.

Police and security tightly guard many areas. Fortunately, even if you can't get inside, you can get views from the street or a drone if you have one. A prime example of a place such as this is the old Raging Waters Waterpark. In its glory days, Raging Waters had one of the first wave pools in the world. Its 17 acres of fun attracted thousands of families every summer. It changed names several times, going by Seven Peaks, Wild Wave, and Raging Waters.

In 2018, the city opted not to renew the waterparks contract, ending its nearly forty years of operation. If the city were to renovate the park, it would cost upwards of $25 million. At least one investor has backed out of the project due to the high renovation cost. While the park sits abandoned and rotting, the city is working to find a new use for the abandoned 17-acre property. Right now, the project seems to be on hold.

Once easily explored and hardly posted, it now has 24/7 security. While security won't officially let you walk through the abandoned park, they will let you take photos through the fence and fly a drone over the property. Make sure you watch your battery levels, for they will not allow you to retrieve the drone if it crashes/lands within the property. Even through the fence, the waterpark is stunning. A grand waterslide tower beckons you to the property. Bits and pieces of the paint have chipped and cracks are seen throughout the wooden support beams. These slides stand tall amongst the backdrop of the mountains, looming like some sort of monument to times gone by. Some pools have partially filled with water, creating a green swamp-like liquid. Weeds and garbage float on top of the surface of these once pristine pools.

I was fortunate to visit the waterpark roughly a month before it shut down. It was in poor condition at the time, with the majority of the waterslides and pools already shut down. In just a few short years, the waterpark went from a center of fun to a center of crime, arson, and mischief. When it was first abandoned, security was lax, allowing almost anyone to explore the property. After several robberies and arson attacks, security ramped up with 24/7 coverage. The area surrounding the park is very sketchy. Behind the park nestled among the railroad tracks is a homeless encampment.

If you decide to visit the park, be sure to go in the daylight hours. You are welcome to view the park from the abandoned lot and I suggest that's where you stay. While it may be tempting to trespass, you will most certainly run into security. I have spoken with security on multiple visits and they are always exceptionally friendly and accommodating as long as you follow the rules. Who knows, they just might let you in!

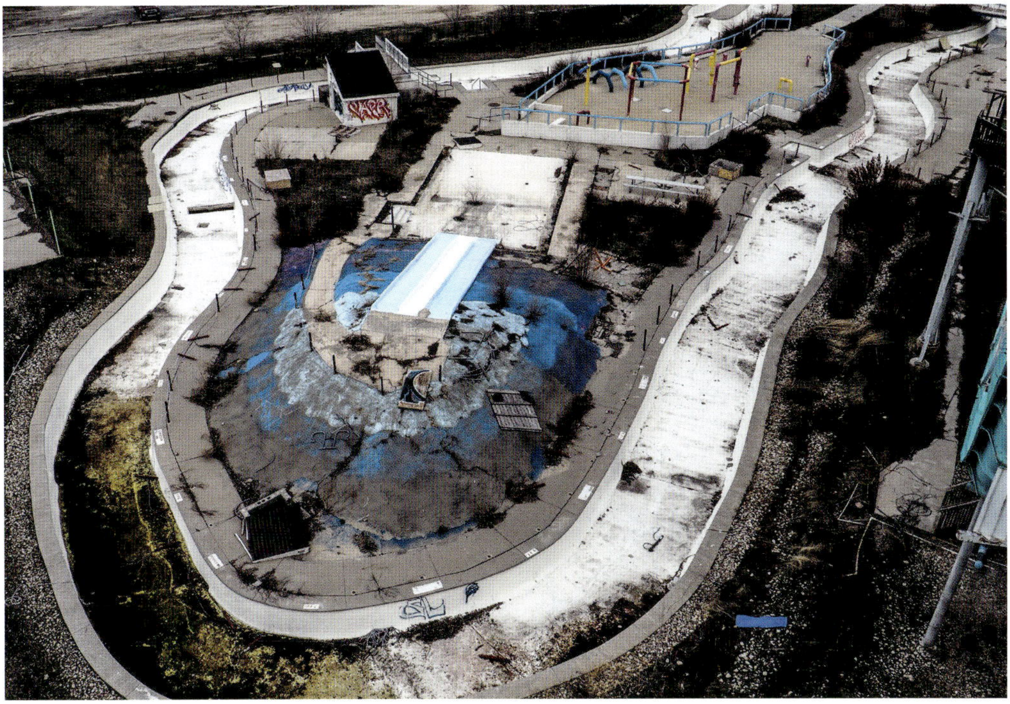

Abandoned lazy river.

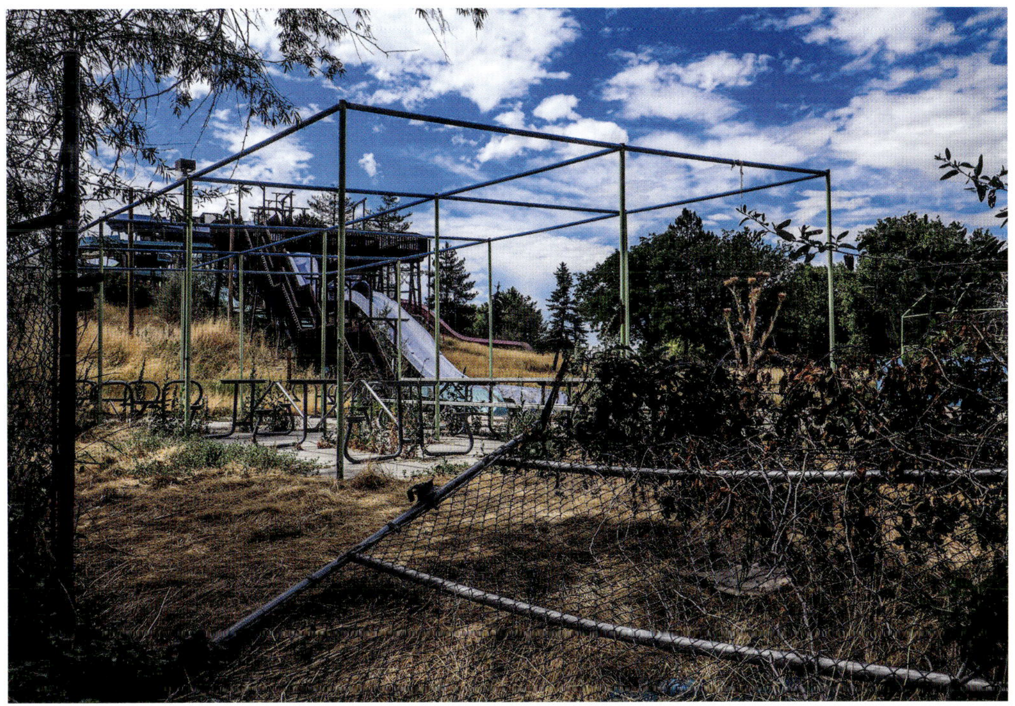

The lure of the abandoned world will forever pull me in.

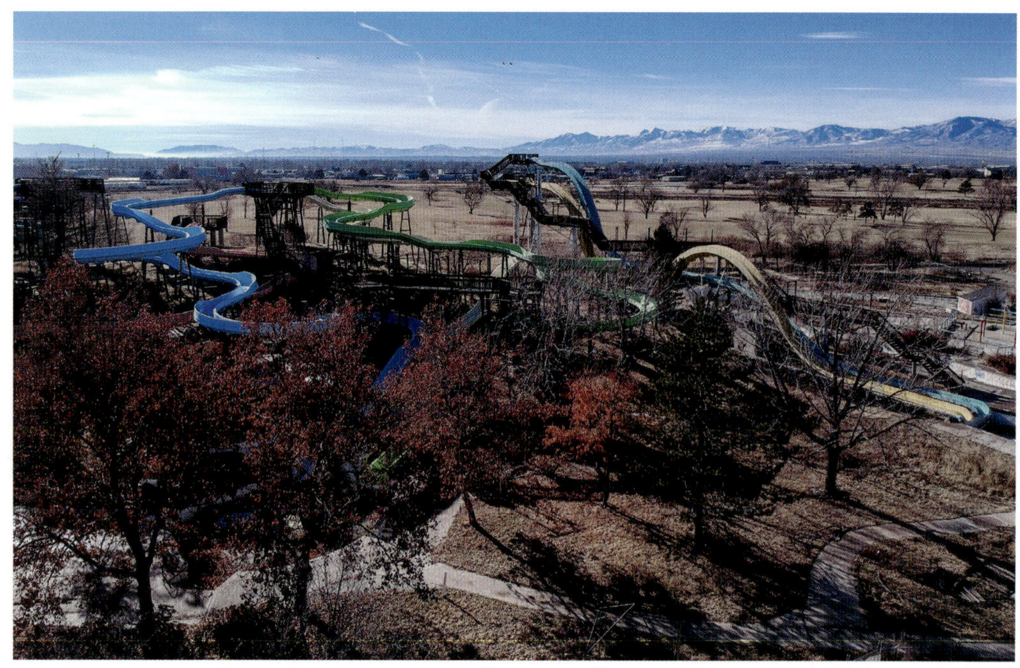

A drone is helpful for locations like this.

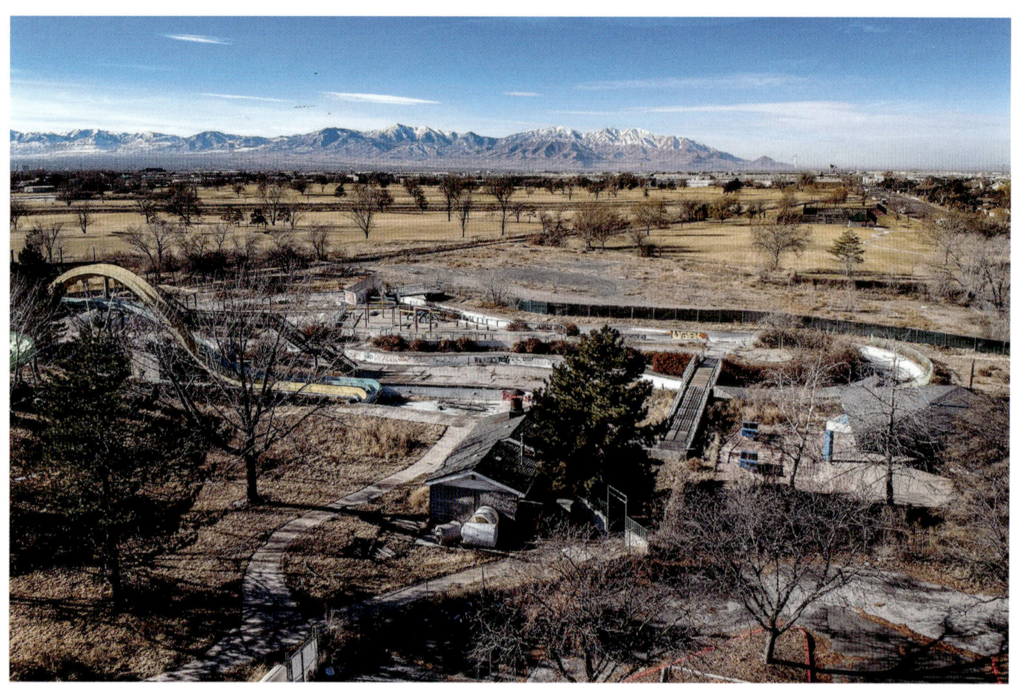

West-facing.

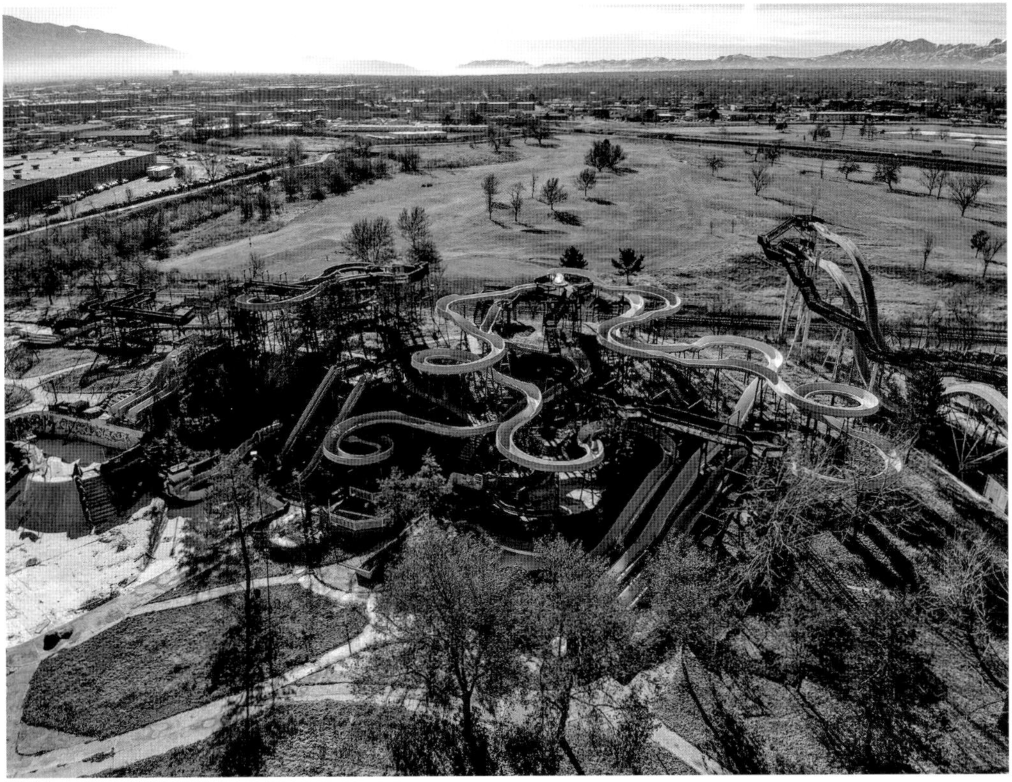

Once a center for fun, now a center for crime.

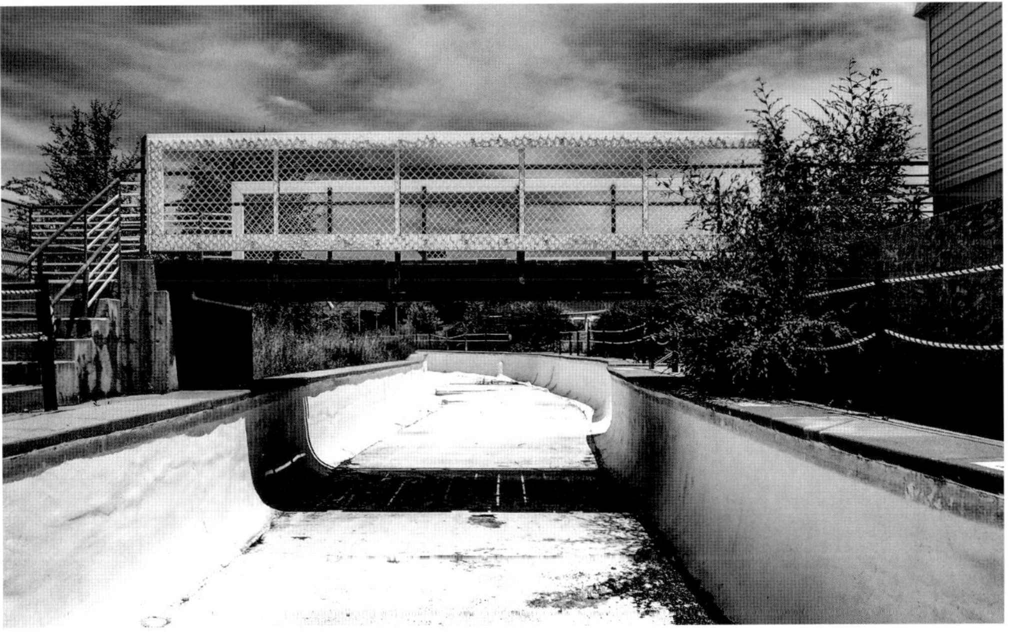

River crossing.

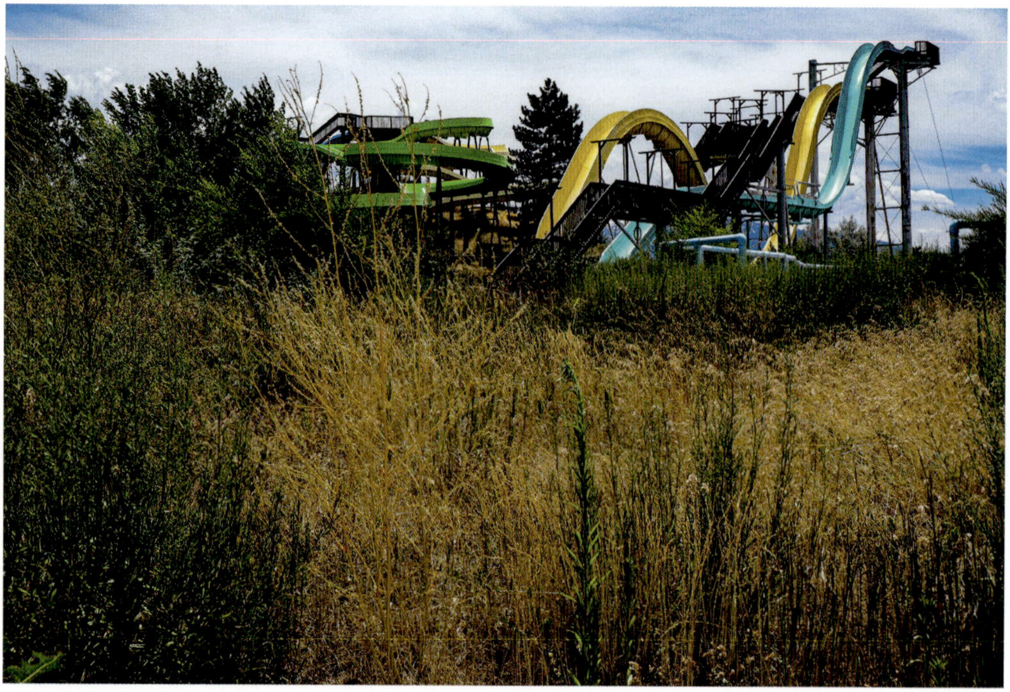

Mother Nature takes over.

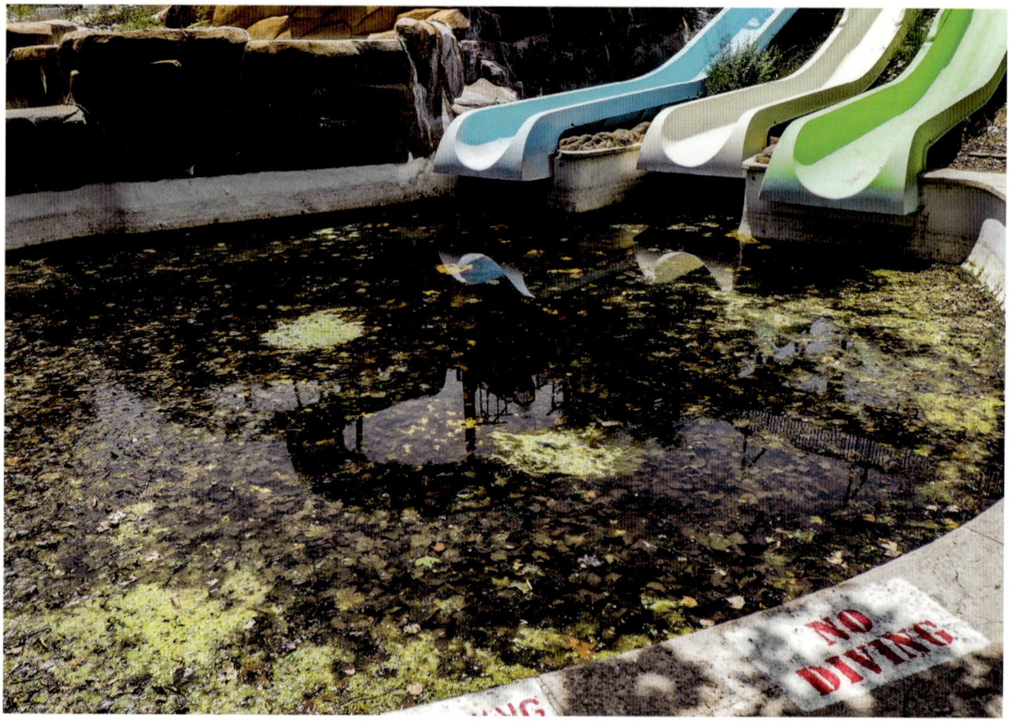

No diving.

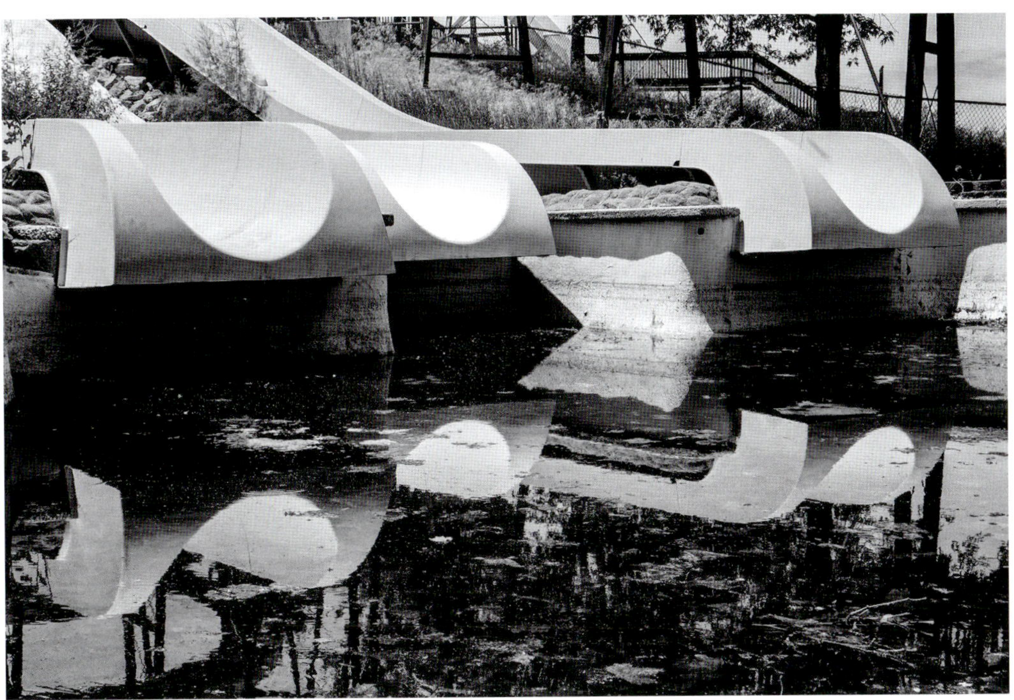

Waterslide reflection.

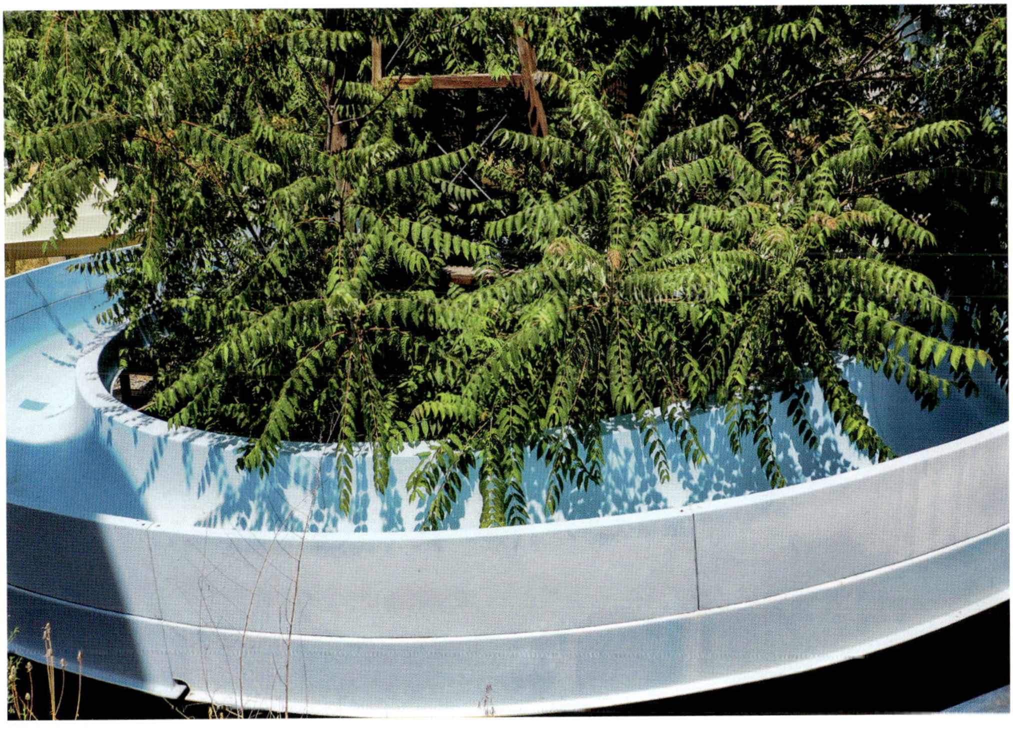

It almost feels tropical here.

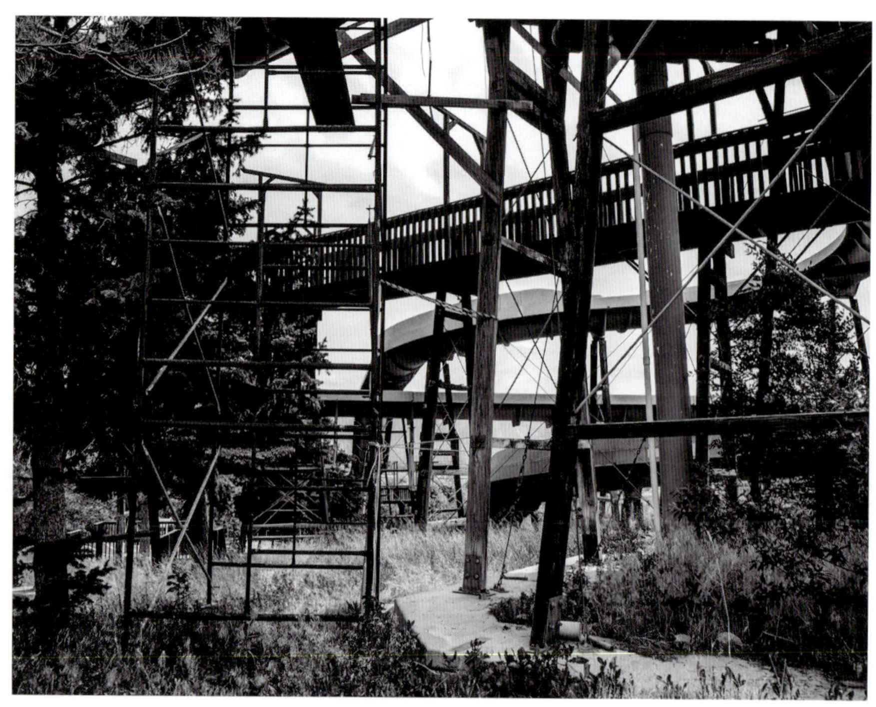

Scaffolding has been left behind from forgotten repairs.

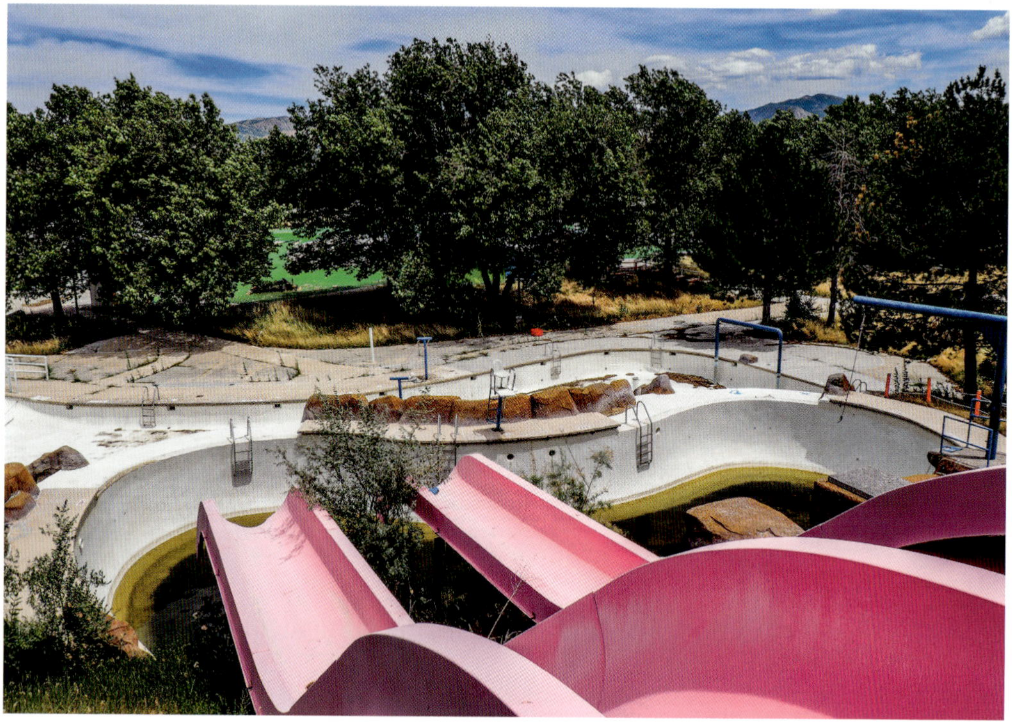

Slides sit dormant awaiting guests that will never return.

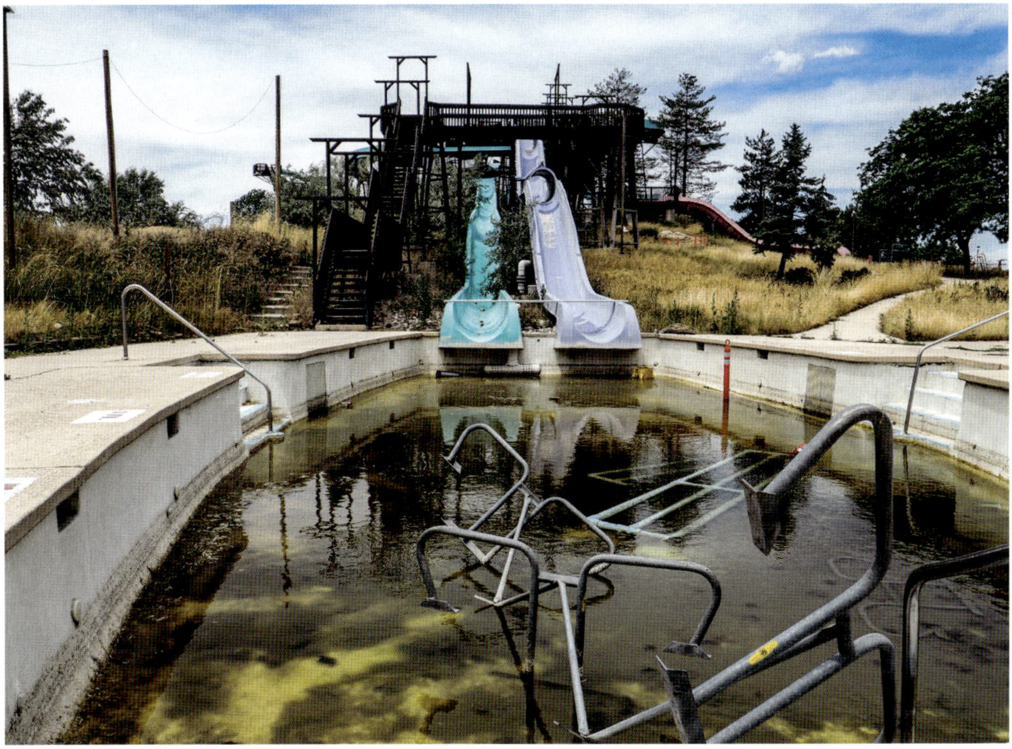

Green lagoon.

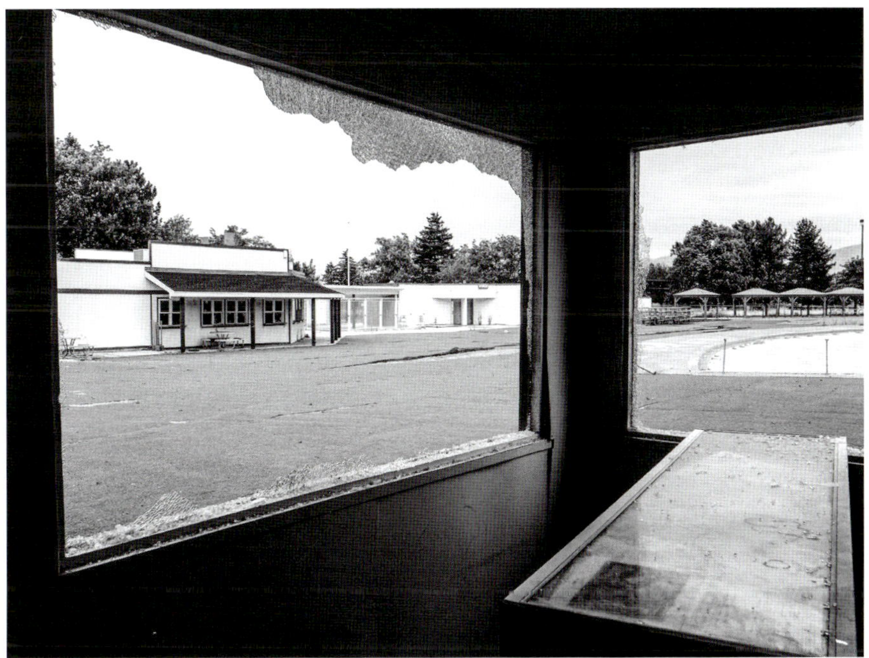

Broken dreams.

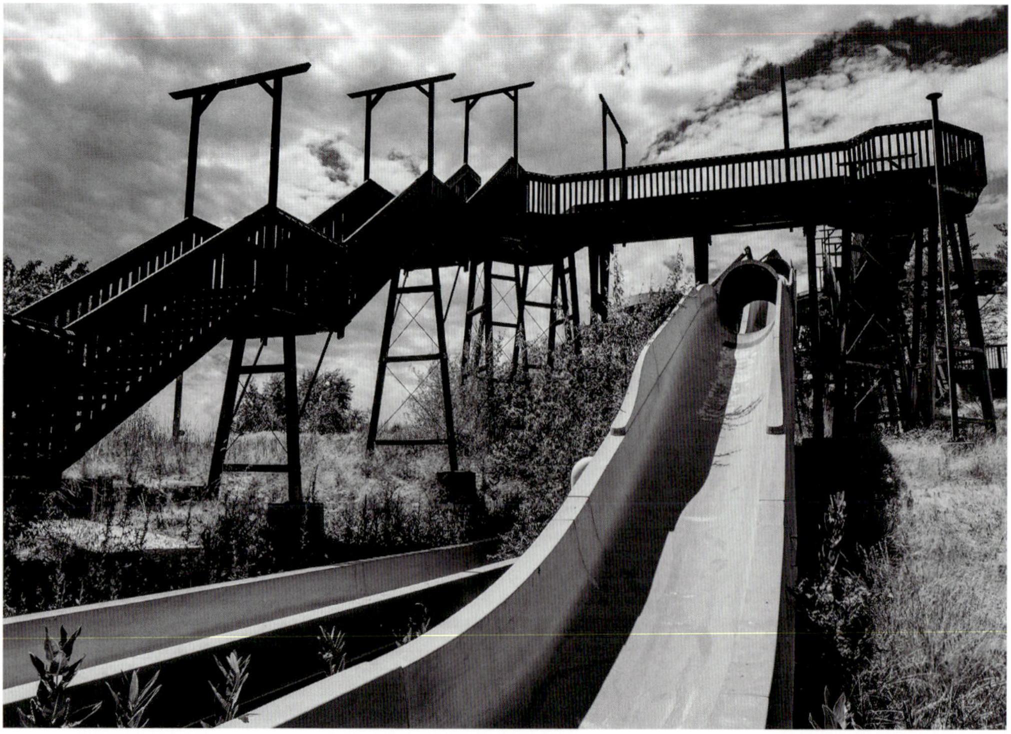

Hellslide.

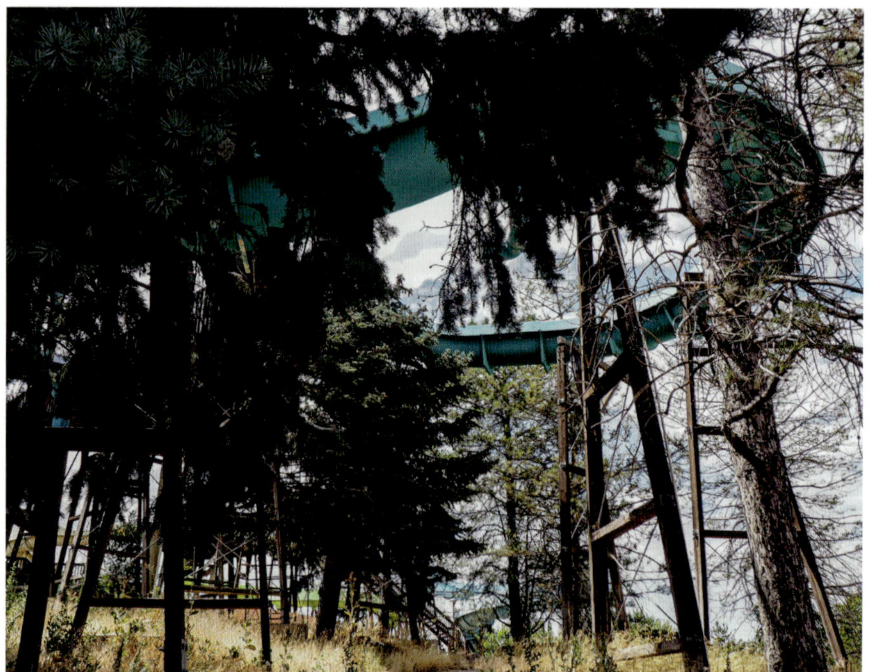

Hidden in the trees.

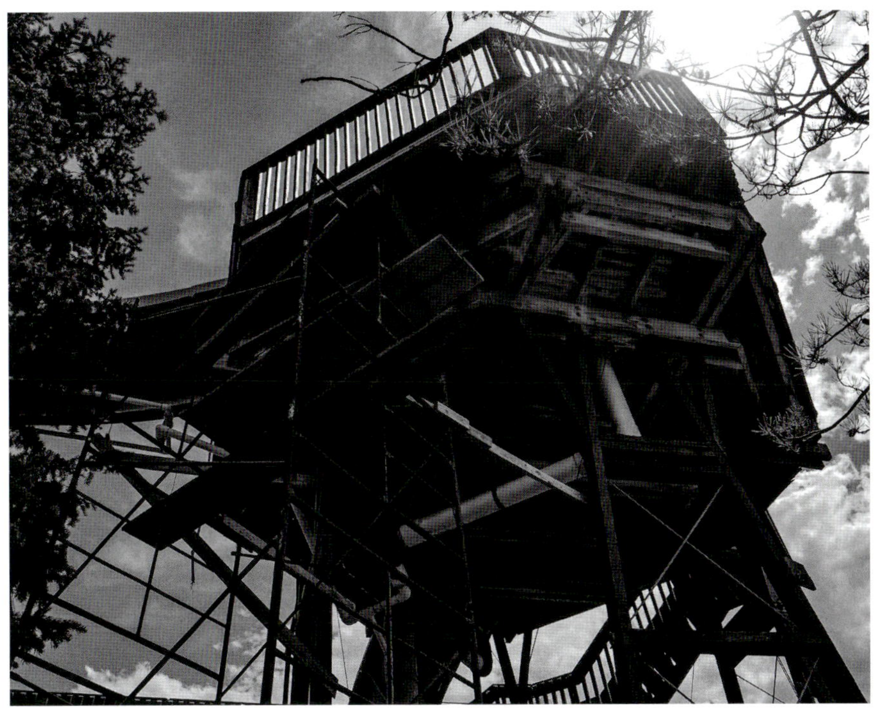

Looming tower.

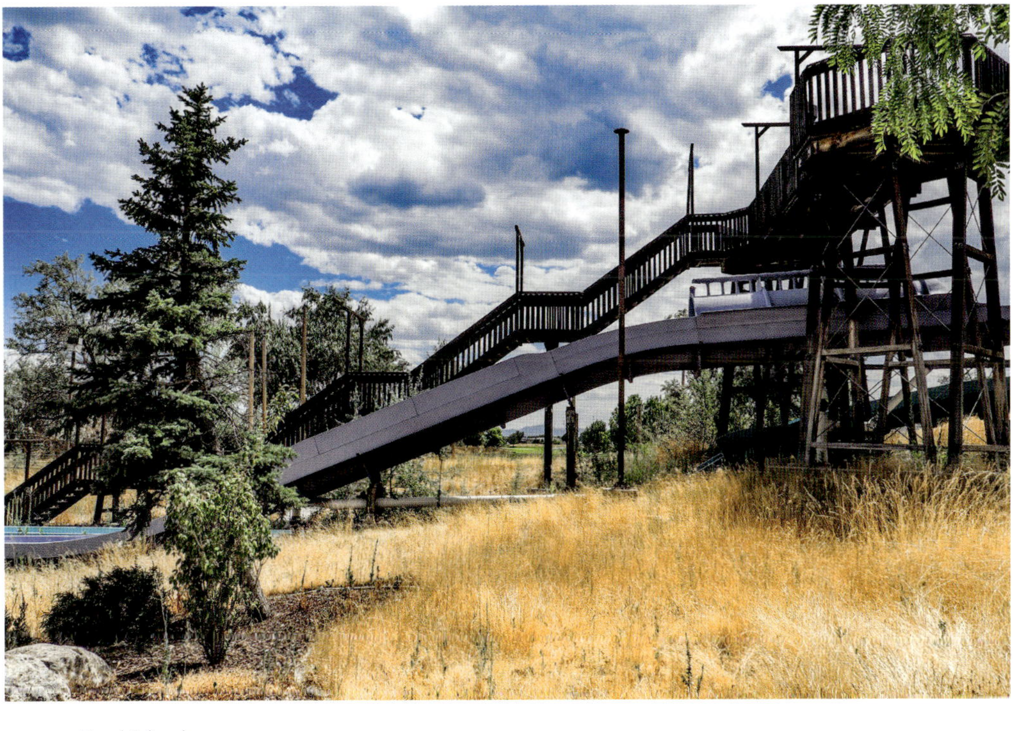

Zombieland.

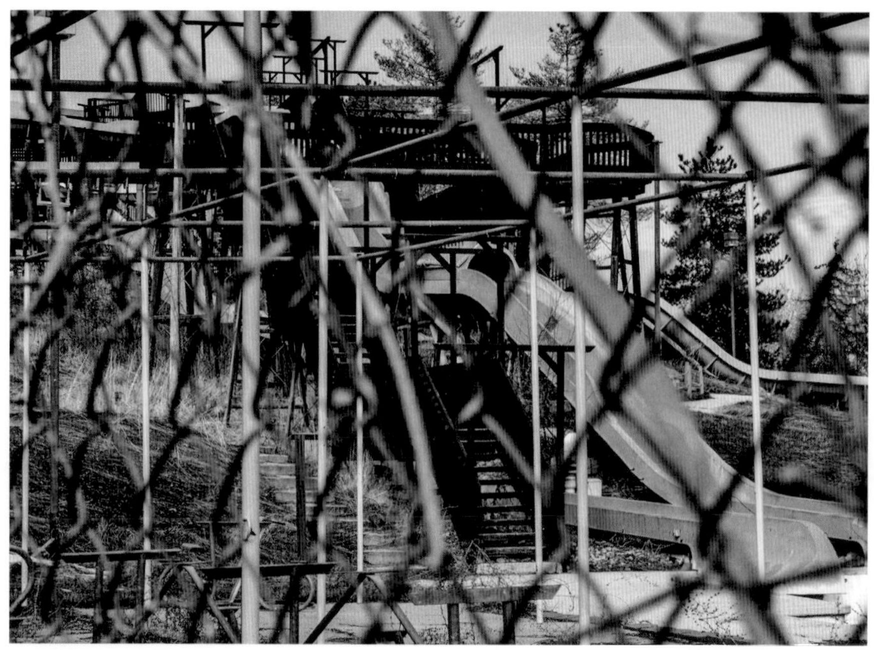

Fenced in.

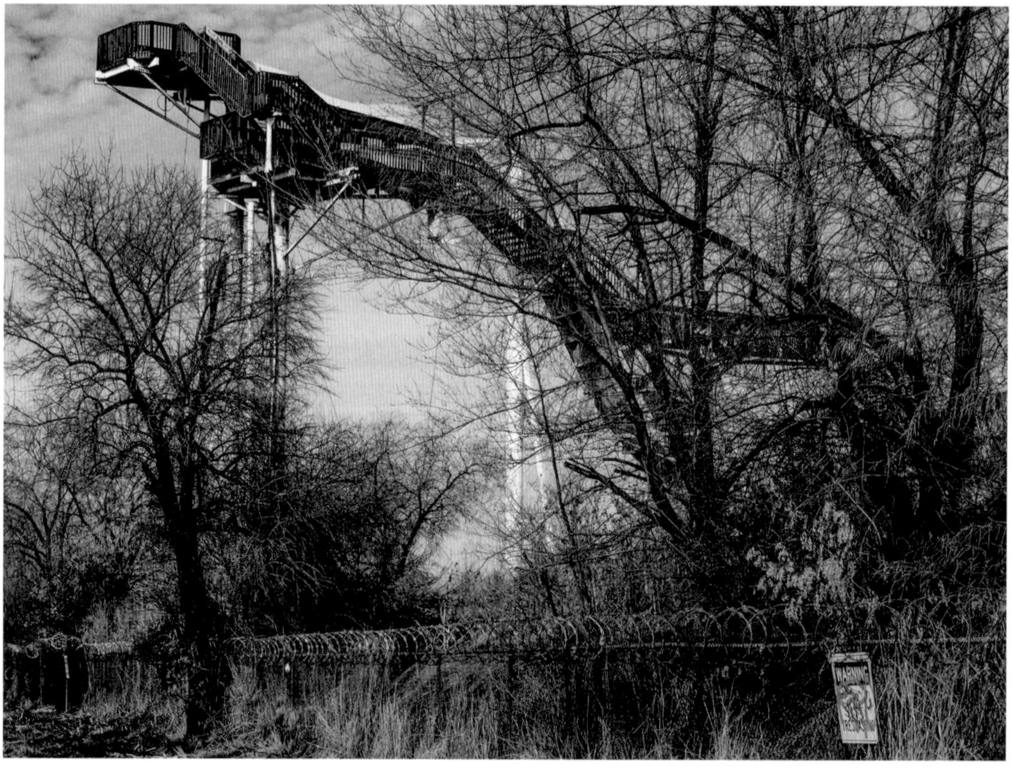

Barbed wire warning.

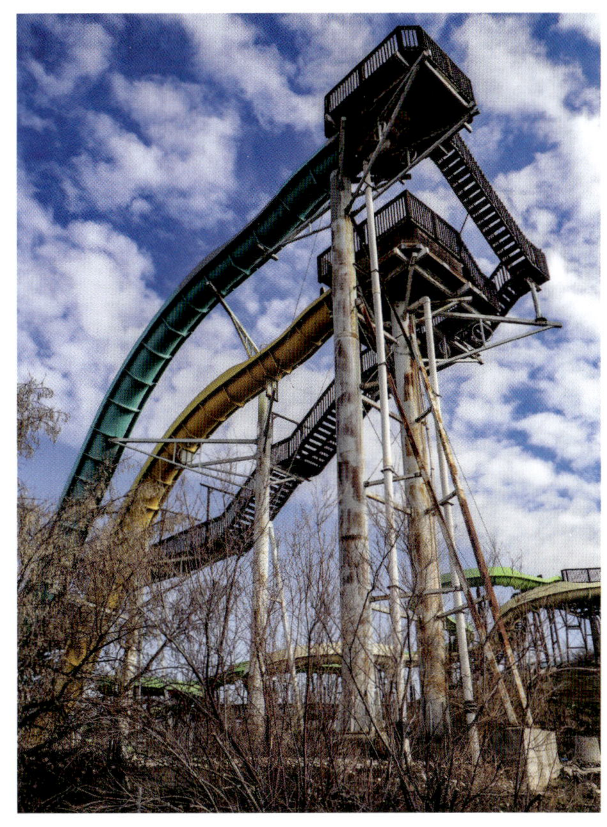

Right: Monuments of fun.

Below: A cold day in Hell.

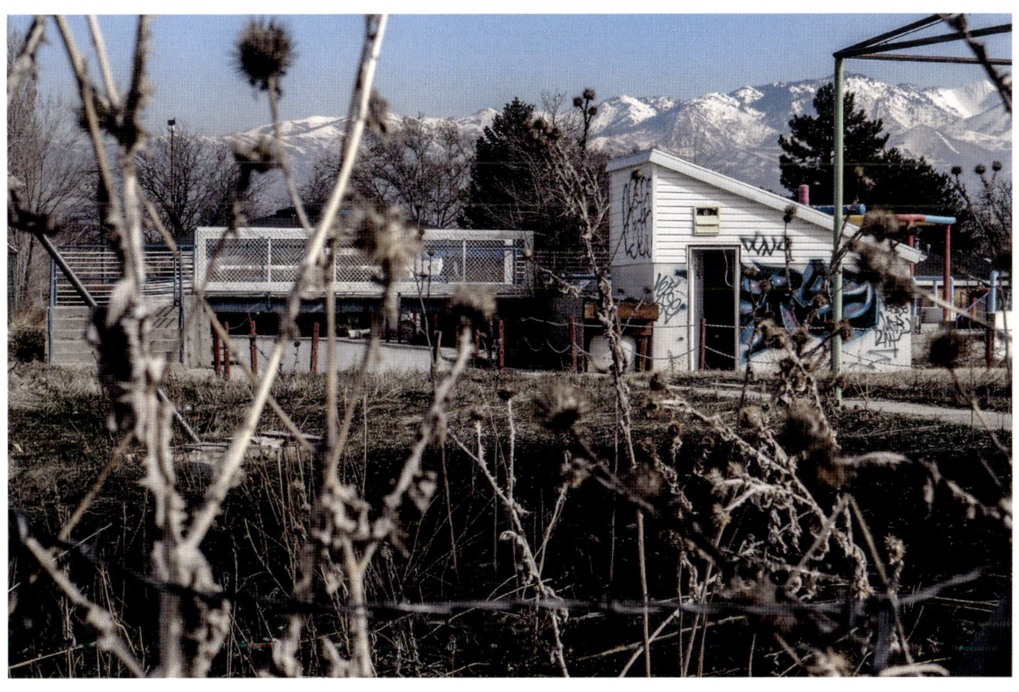

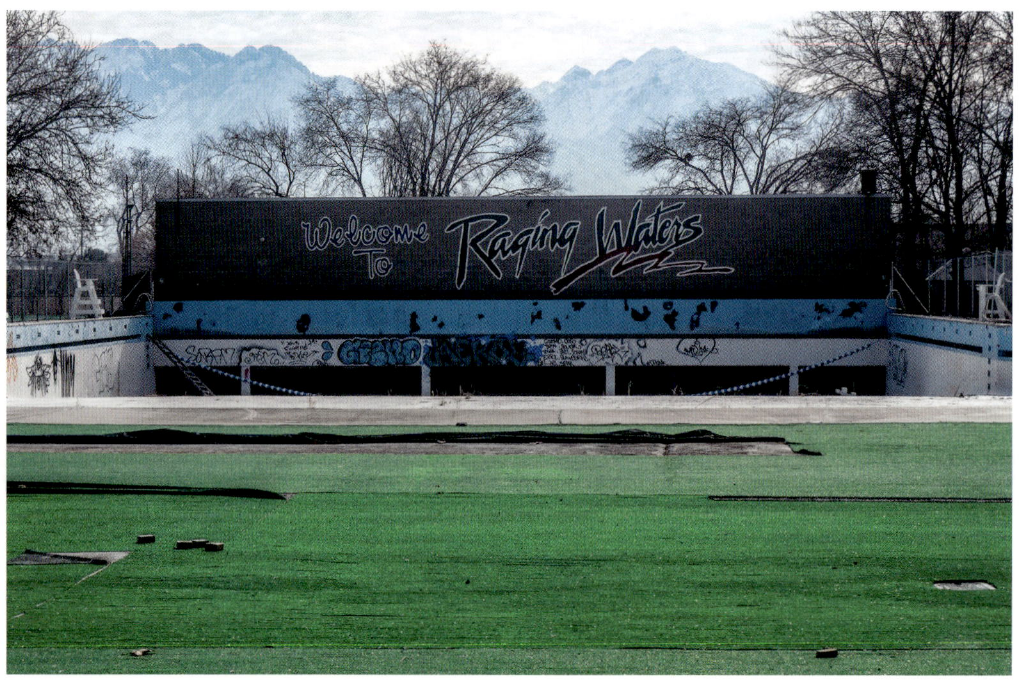

Raging waters.

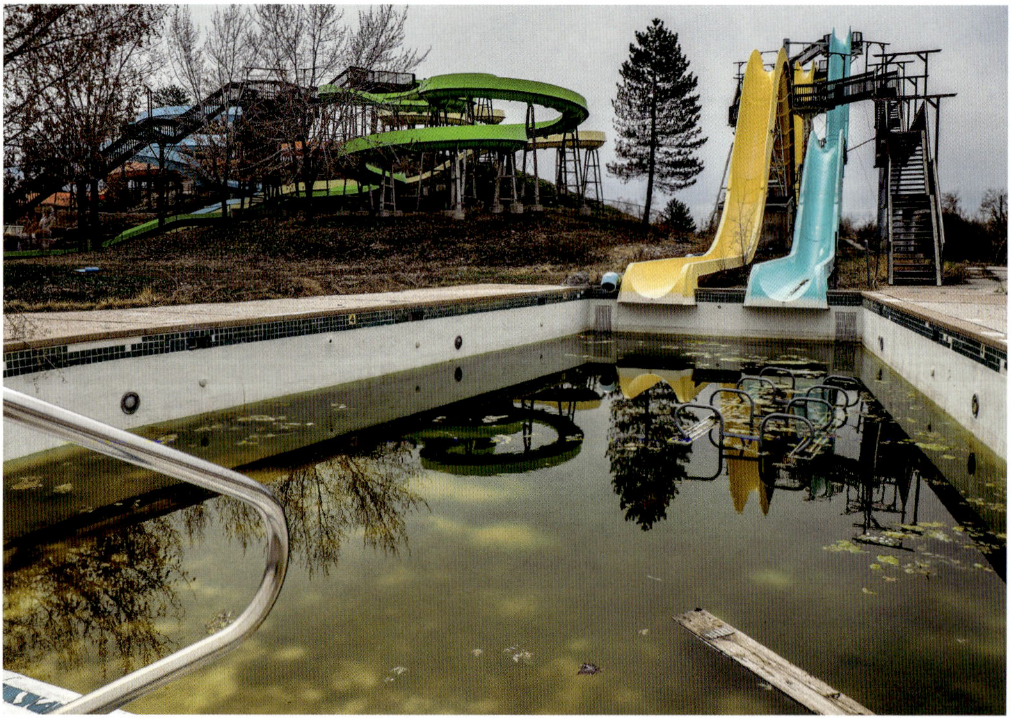

Swamp slide.

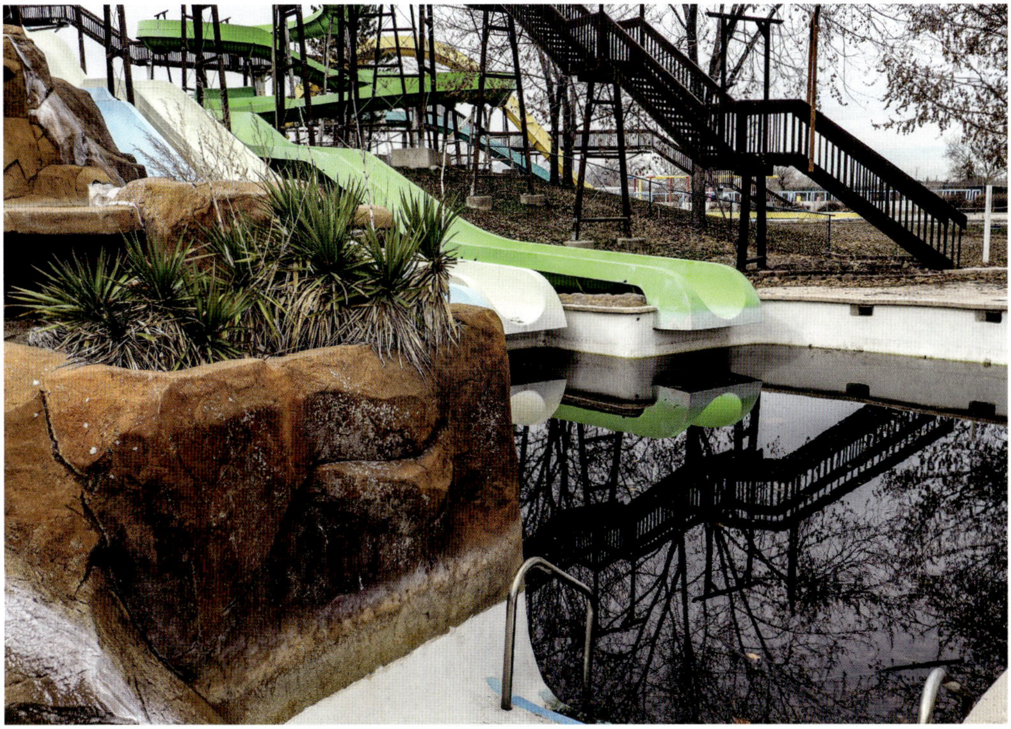

Black lagoon.

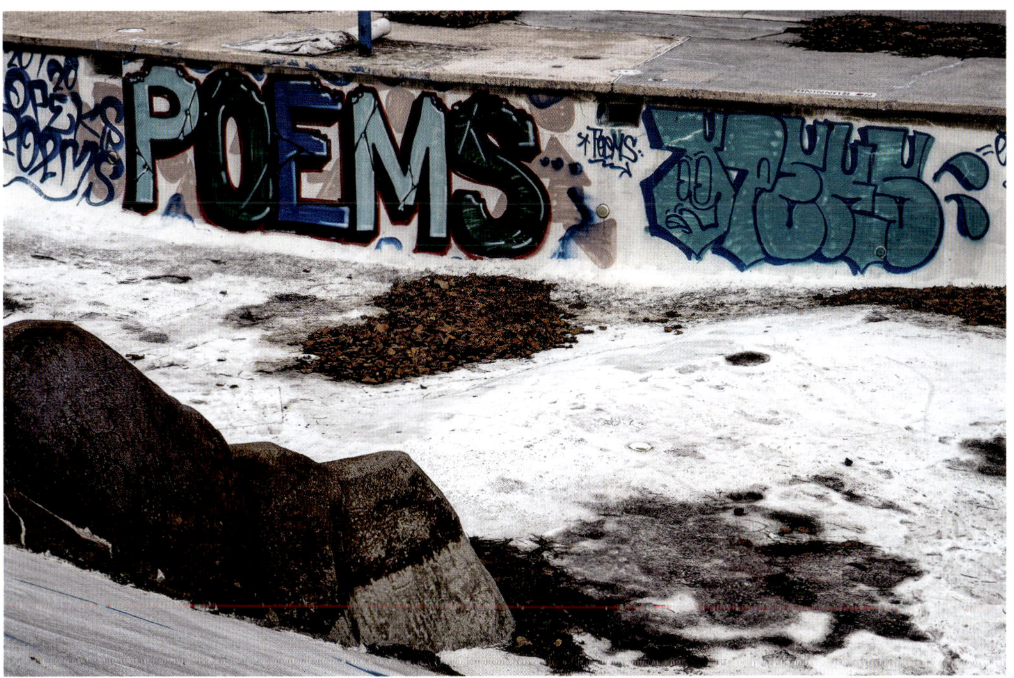

Urban poems.

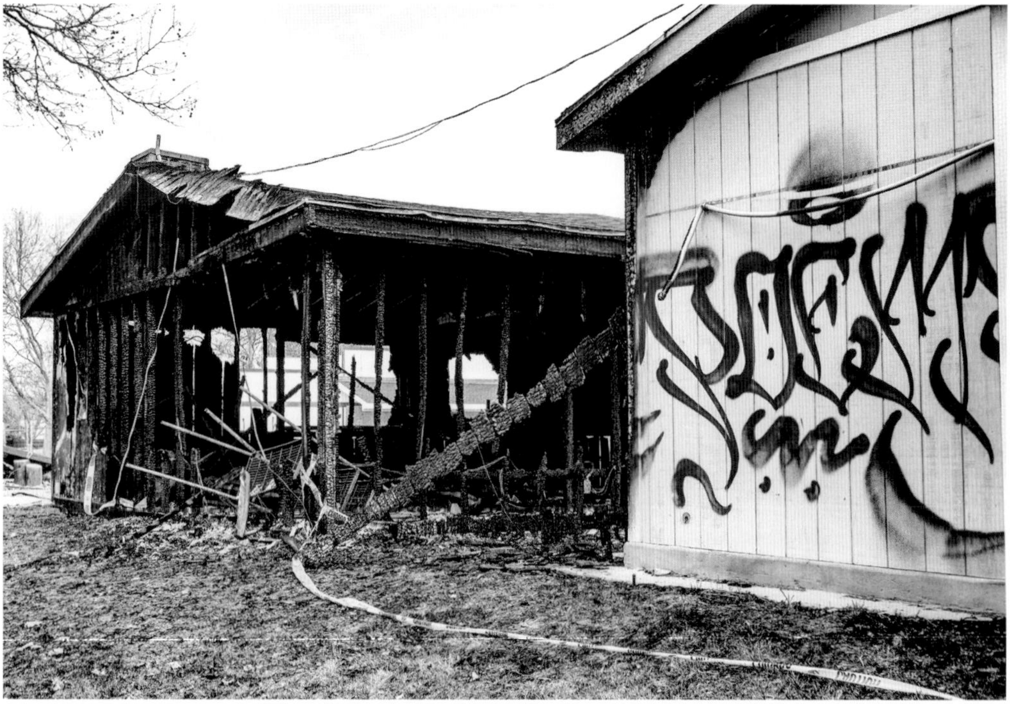

Evidence of arson.

Photograph of a photographer being photographed (Jamie).

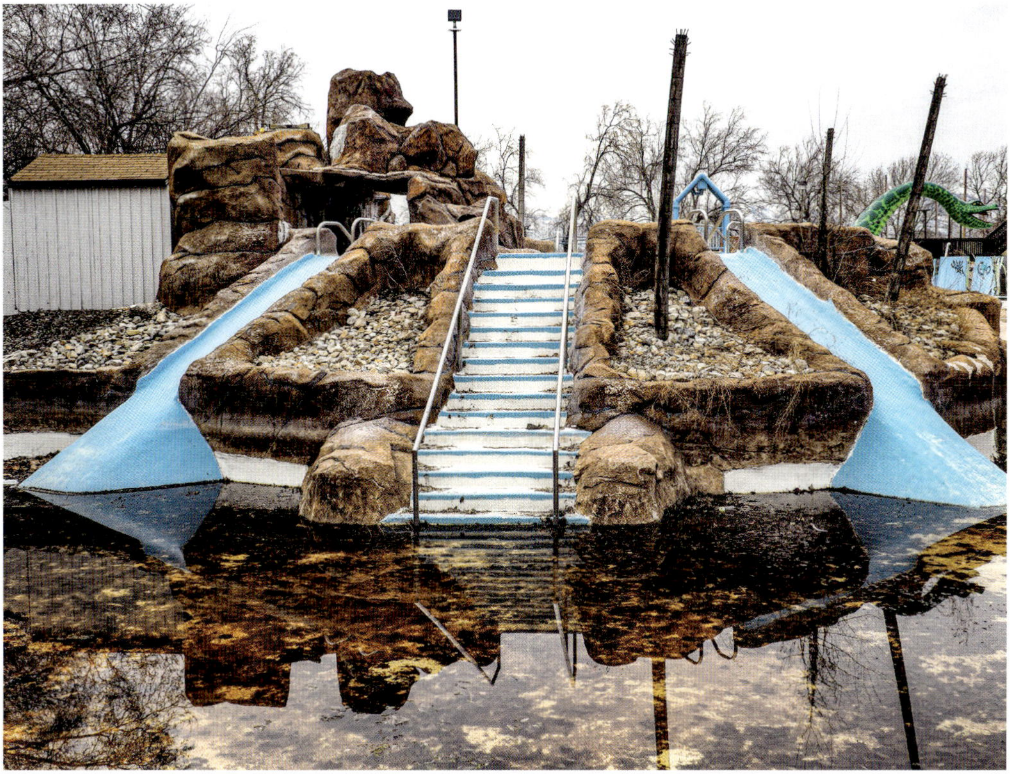

Above: Sea monsters.

Right: Chair of despair.

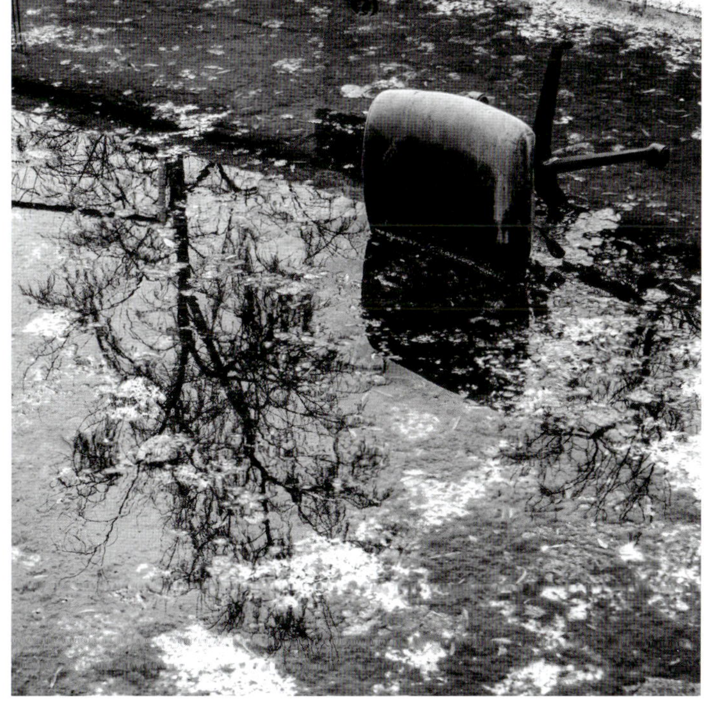

9

Cisco

Just outside of Green River lies the ghost town of Cisco. Cisco sprung to life in the 1880s as a service station to the Denver and Rio Grande Railroad. Trains would be fueled and serviced here as they made their way across the vast expanse of the west. The town thrived for several decades with a maximum population of roughly 200 people. In the 1950s, the decline began. Steam engines were replaced by diesel, thus eliminating the need for them to be serviced in Cisco. Even with this new technology, the town held on. Travelers would stop here to refuel and recharge. Johnny Cash even wrote a song about Cisco, entitled "Cisco Clifton's Filling Station." The song discusses what life was like in the town as it began to decline. The construction of a new highway ultimately killed Cisco. Travelers no longer passed through the town. Eventually, the last gas station shut down and so did the town.

Nowadays, Cisco has become an art installation of sorts. A lone resident moved in and has made the place their own. Being so close to the highway, many people visit Cisco. Evidence of vandalism and graffiti cover the town, directly clashing with the beautiful artwork. After being told stories of suspicious encounters within the town, caution was used when I entered. I encountered no harassment and walked freely among the streets. Beautiful murals and colorful artwork are dispersed throughout the town.

A small post office is seen from main street with a general store just around the corner (it was closed when I visited). A snake run of concrete has been masterfully constructed. It was built by a few creative and dedicated individuals located alongside the vibrant shell of an old bus. Bring your skates, scooter, or skateboard and drop in!

Giving off a burning man vibe, temporary dwellings made out of RVs and creatively restored structures provide housing for various events throughout the year. The town's perimeter is full of abandoned cabins, a service station, rusted-out cars, and various objects strewn about the land. The flat desert landscapes provide for a wonderful backdrop against both grey and blue skies. Railroad tracks aren't far away with trains occasionally passing. While the public is welcome to explore, be sure to follow all posted rules and respect those that still live in the area.

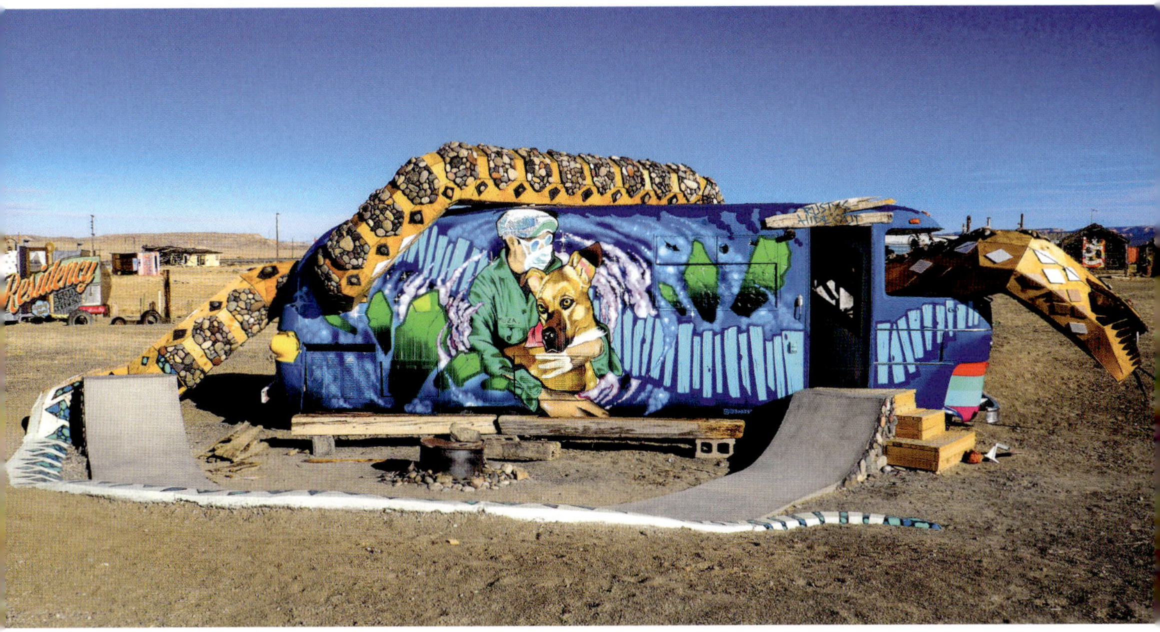

Snake run.

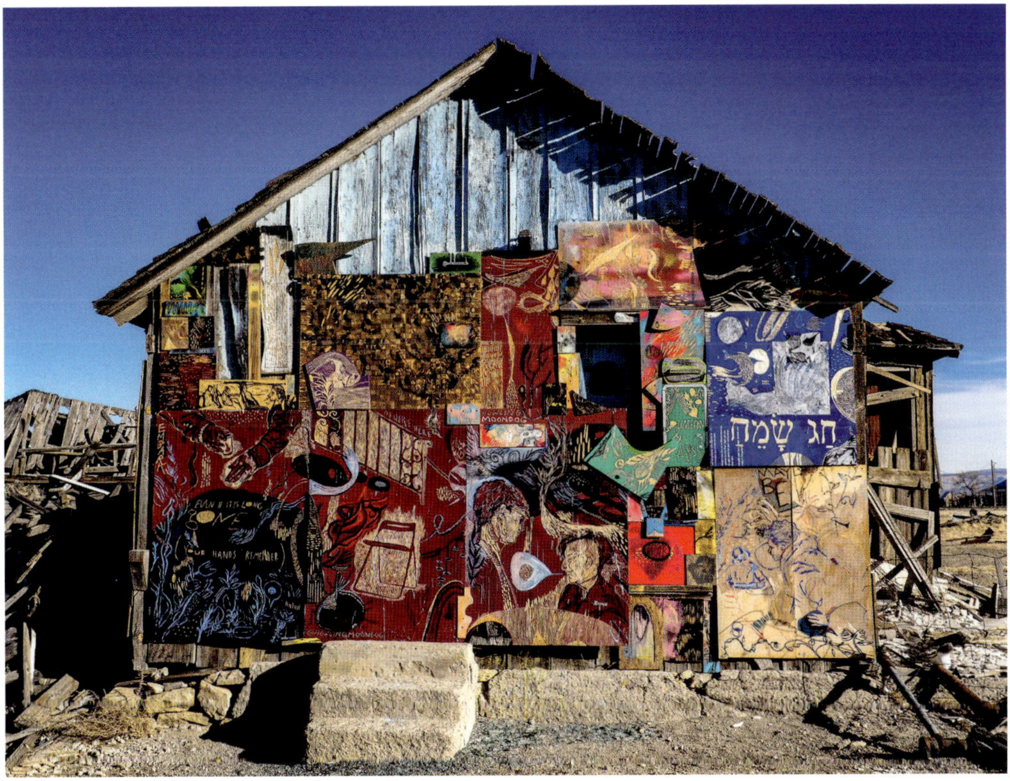

The entire town is a work of art.

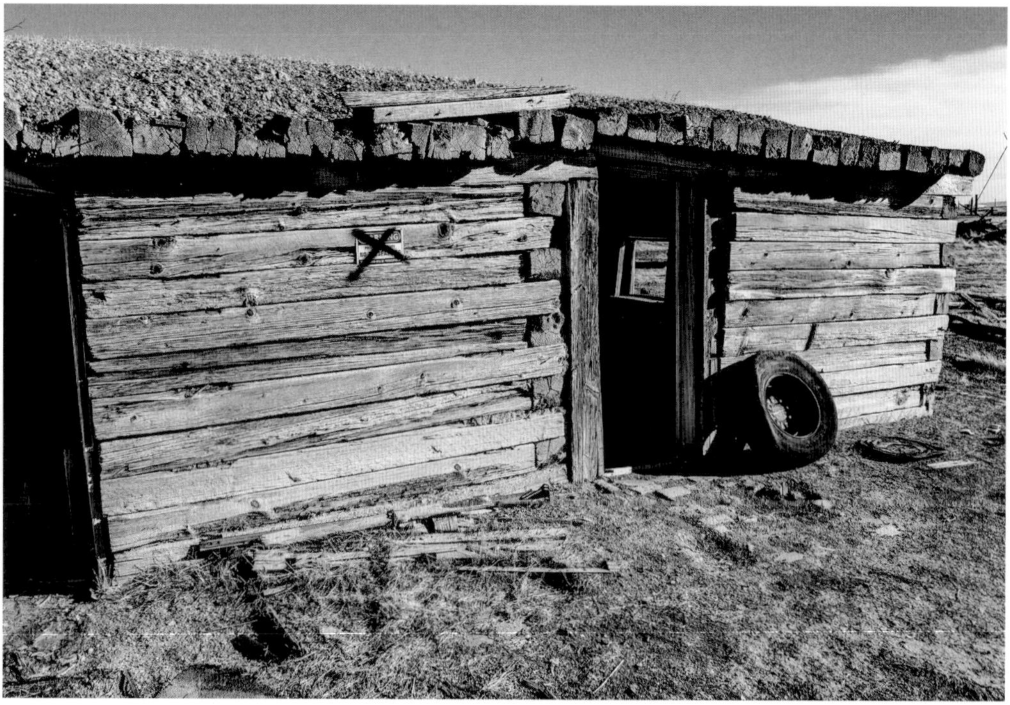

Abandoned cabin.

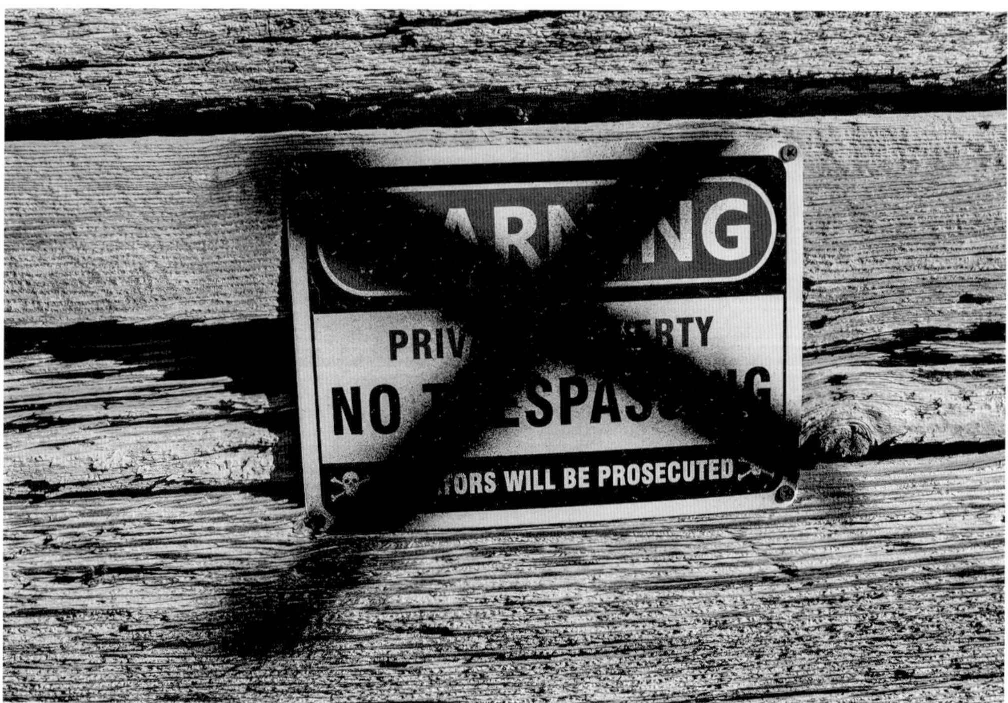

Canceled.

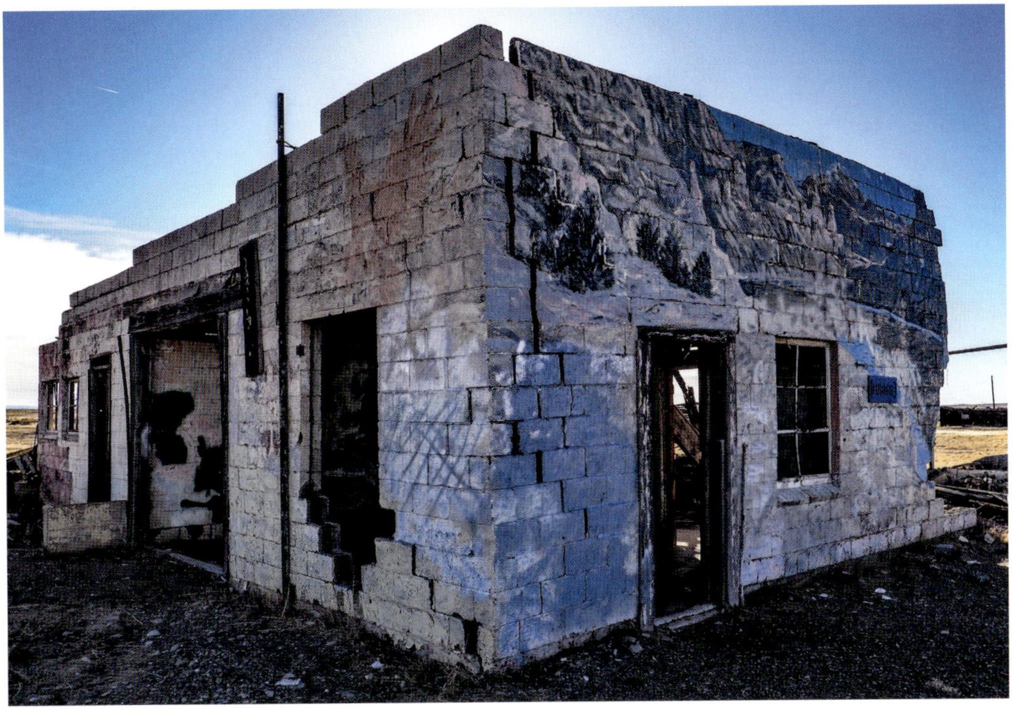

Cisco Clifton's filling station.

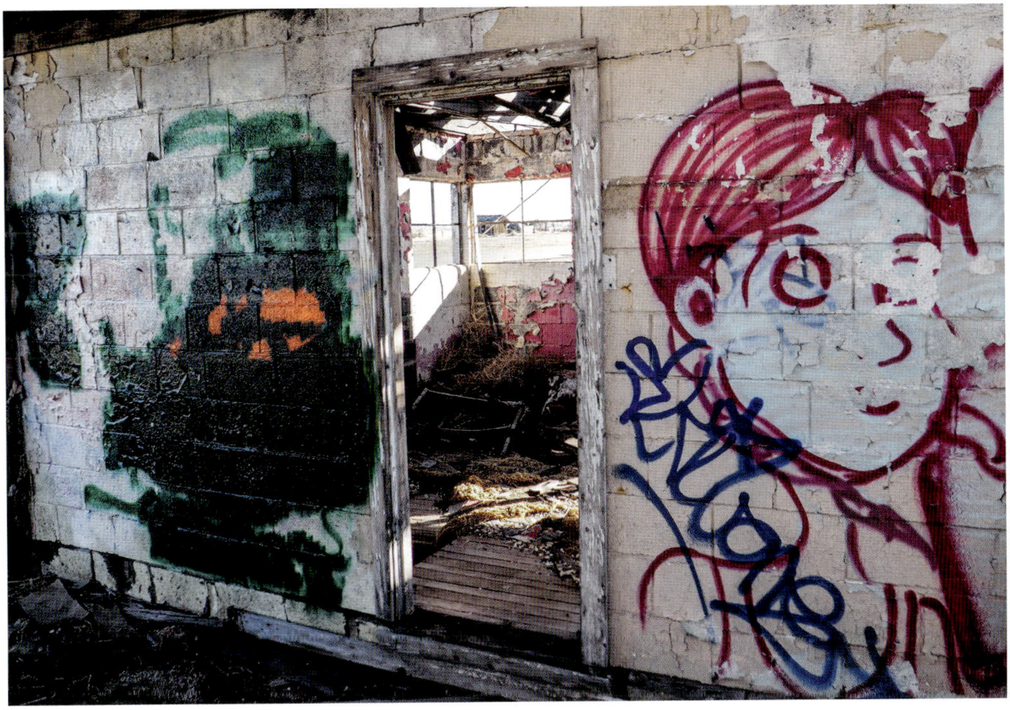

Decayed graffiti.

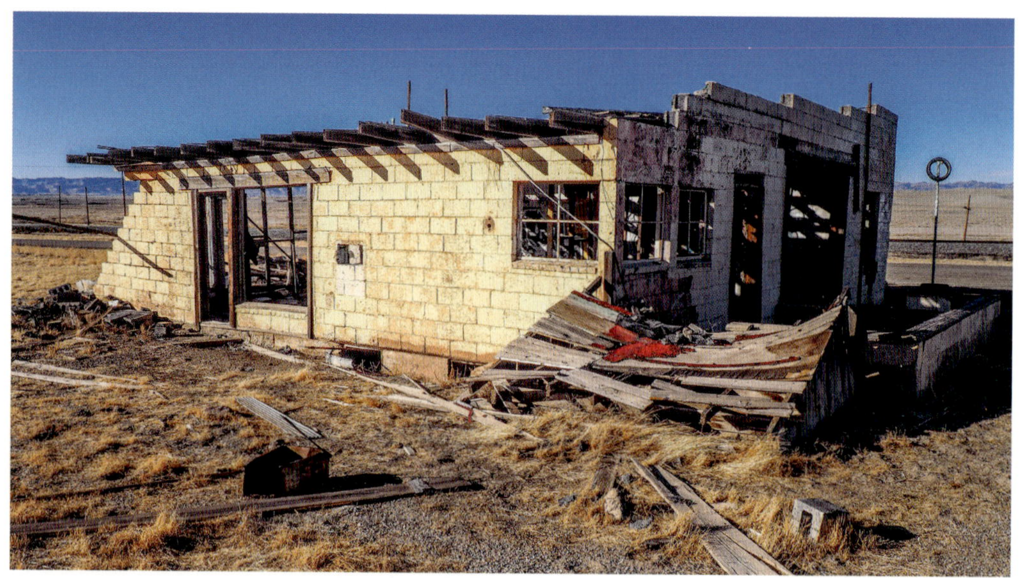

The nearby highway ultimately killed Cisco.

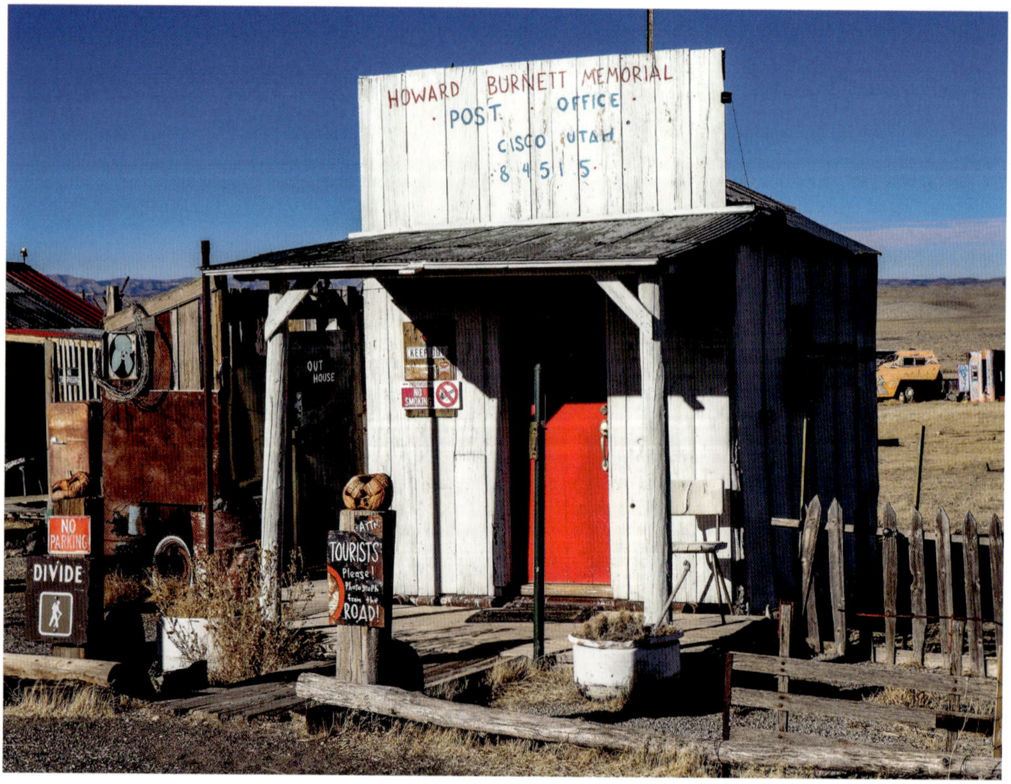

Obey the rules.

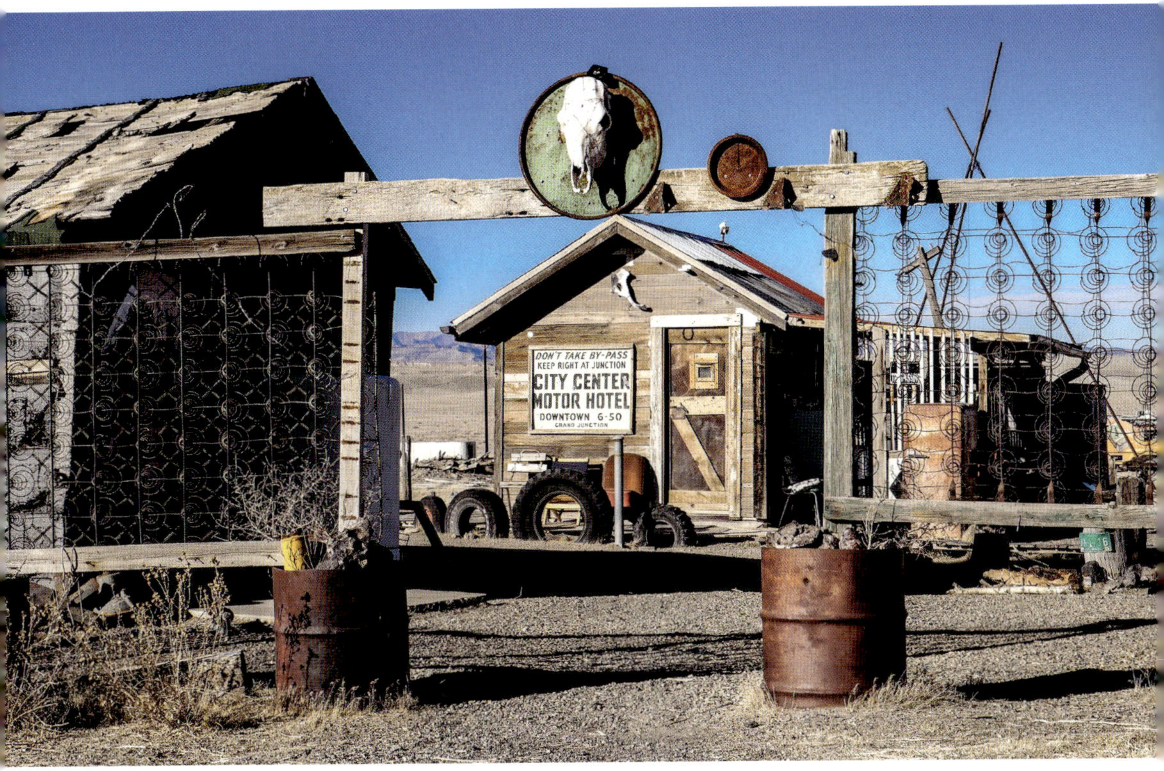

Cattle skulls and shotgun shells.

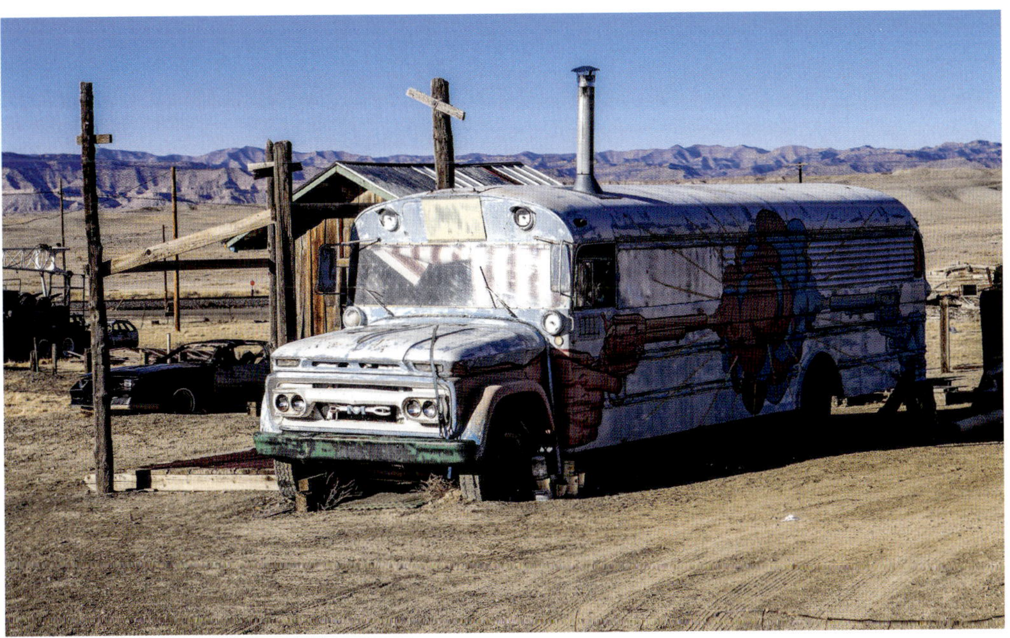

Quickdraw!

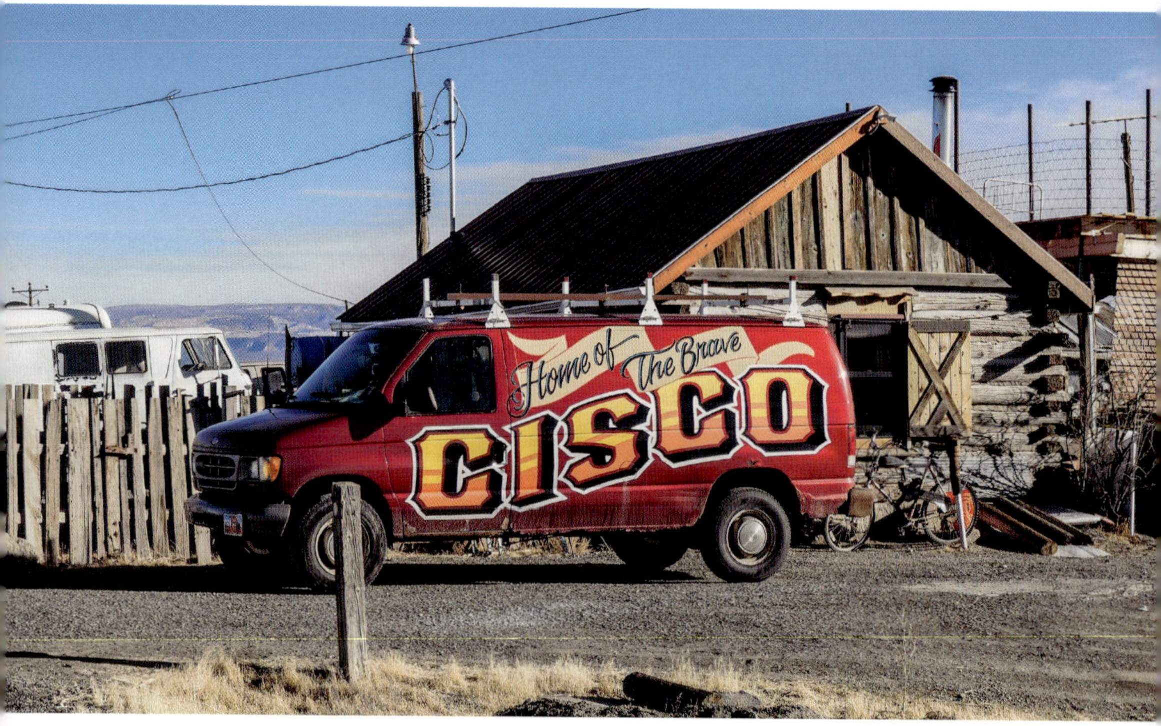

Home of the brave.

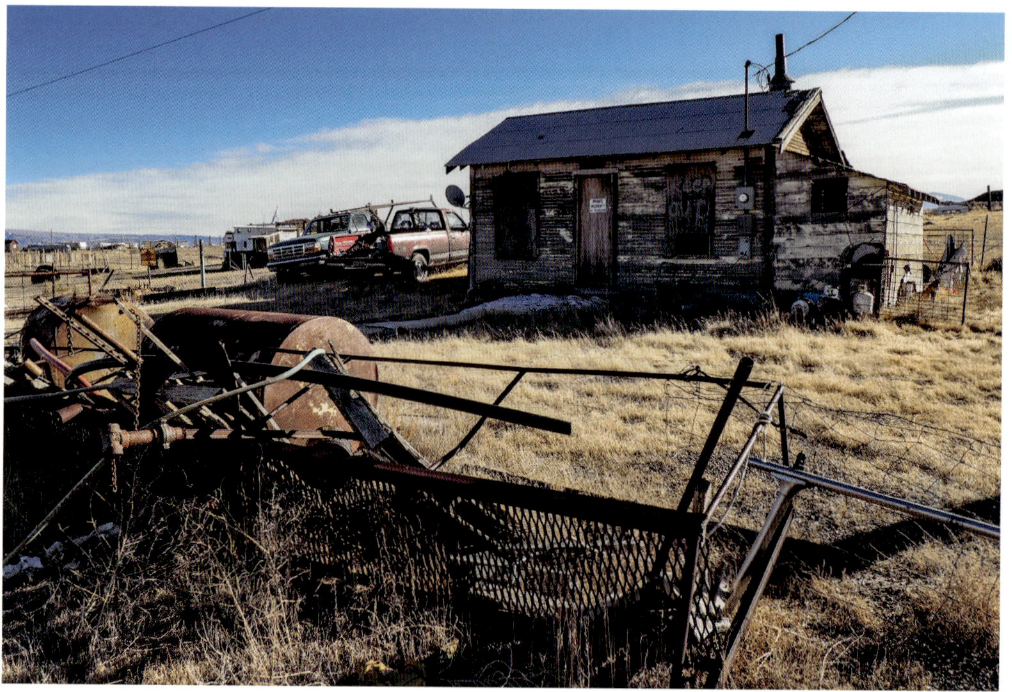

Keep out!

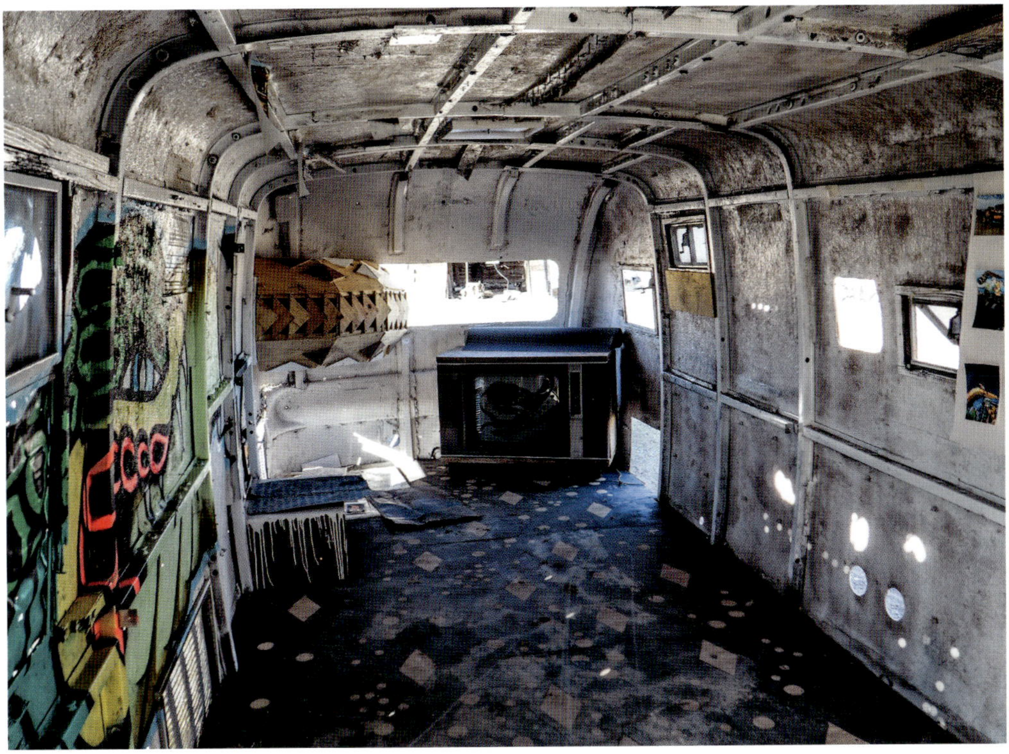

Interior of the snake run bus.

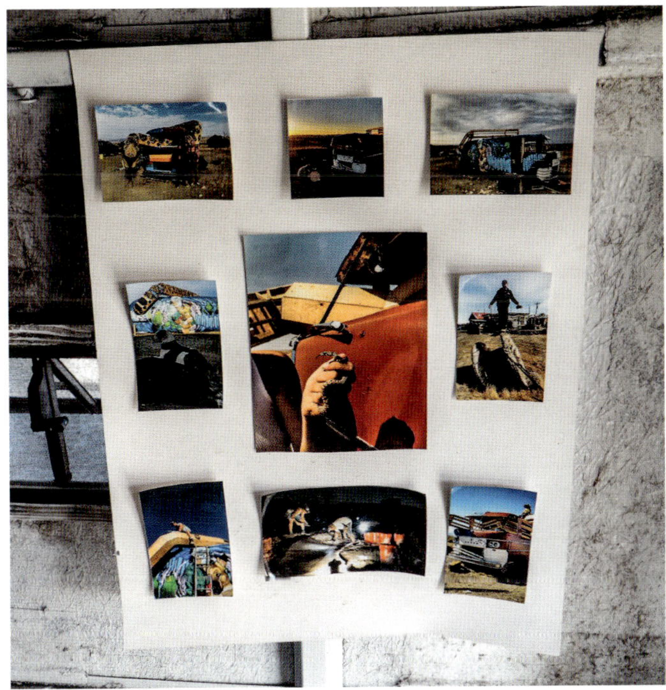

A dedicated group of skaters and artists built this skateable piece of art.

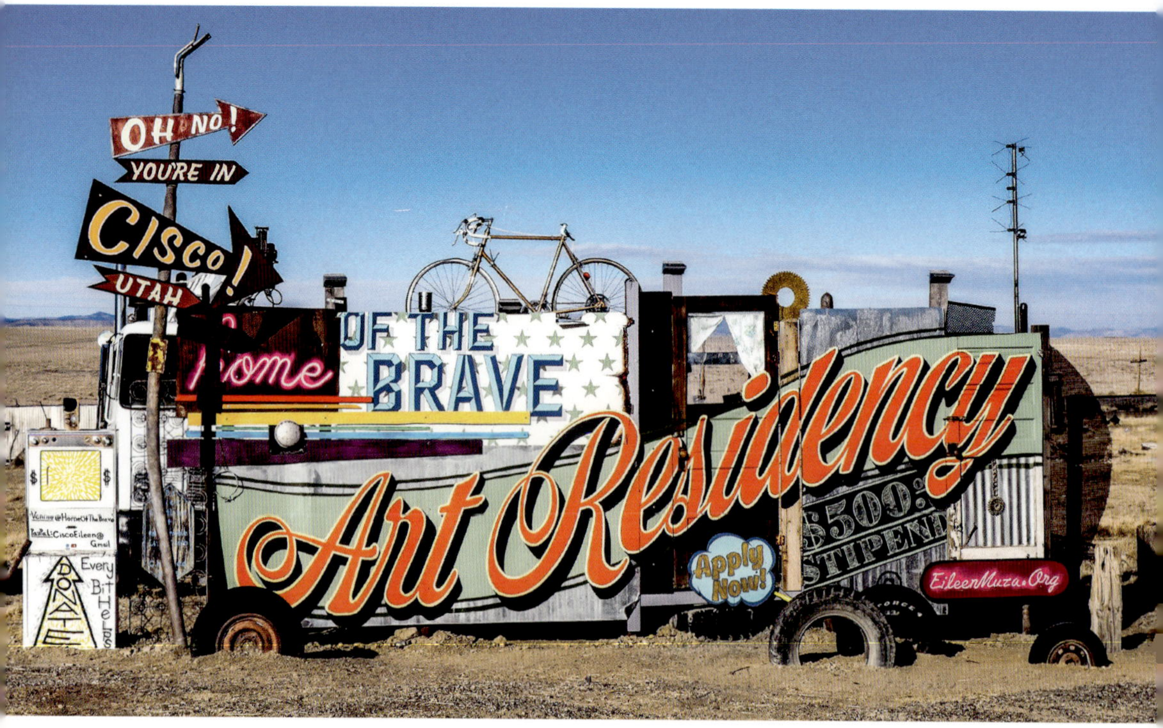

Oh no! You're in Cisco!

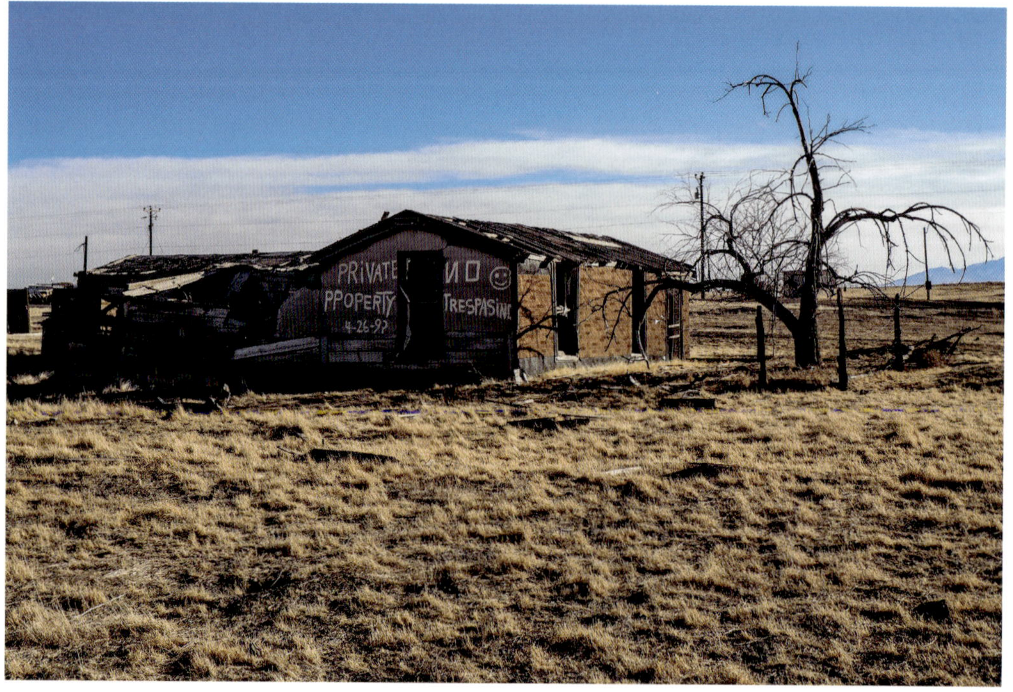

Smile, you're trespassing.

10

Street Photography

Wandering the streets can provide a wealth of knowledge. Things you never noticed before appear in front of your eyes. While I'll admit I'm an amateur at best when it comes to artistic visions of daily life, I do enjoy exploring the urban environment. I never know what I'll find. Bringing a camera makes me feel like I'm a tourist in my own city. Alleys look strange and foreboding with signs of homeless and squatters. The public frightens yet intrigues me. I find myself wondering about the lives of everyone I pass. Where are they headed? What's their story?

As we reach the end of our journey, I hope I've piqued your curiosity. You don't have to go far to discover strange and exciting places. I encourage you to go out and explore on your own. No matter where you live, I can almost guarantee that you can find something you weren't aware existed. All you have to do is look. Remember, never stop exploring!

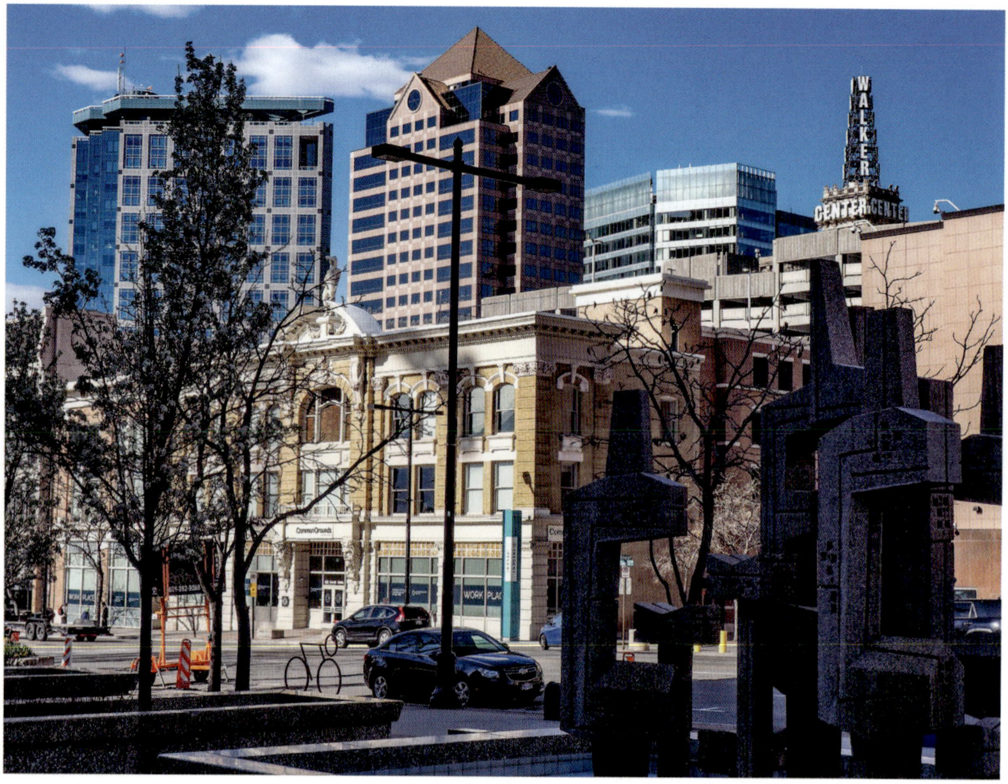

Welcome to Salt Lake City.

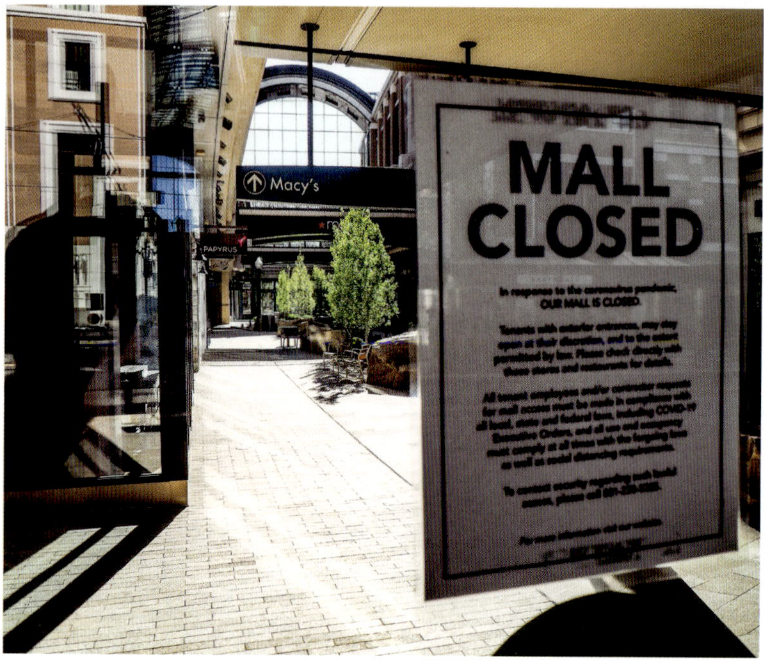

During the first wave of Covid, many malls and businesses shut down.

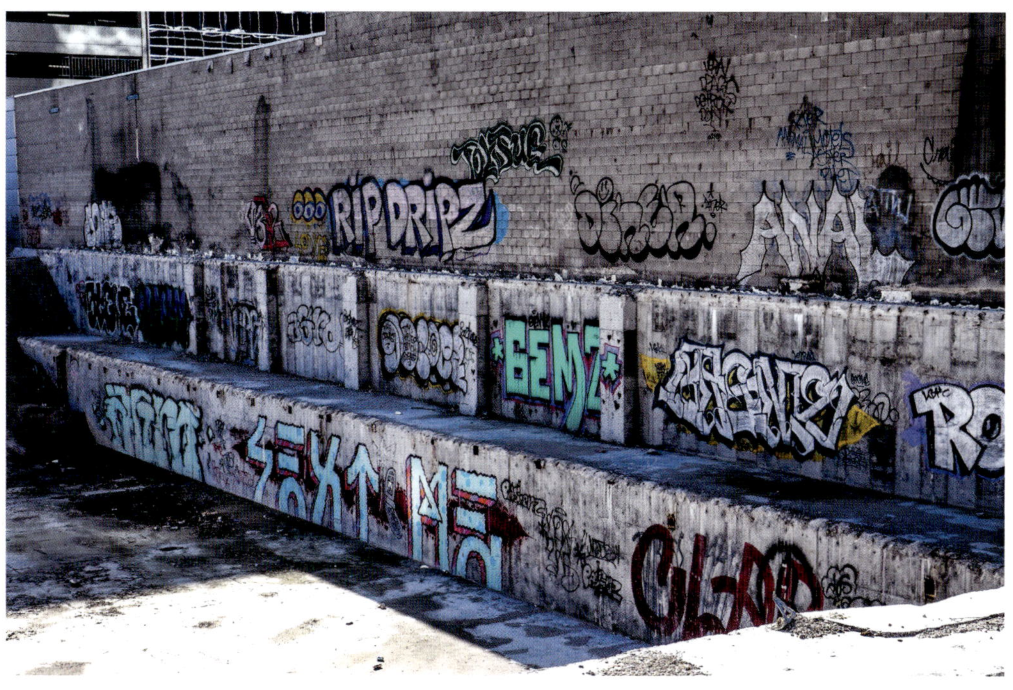

Downtown graffiti.

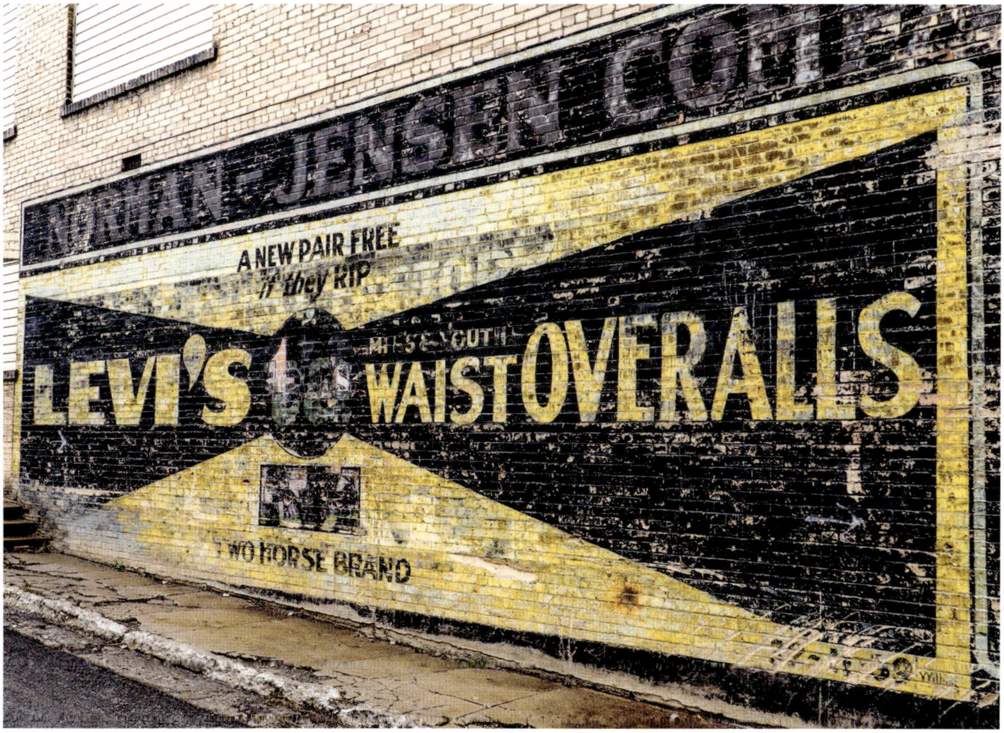

Old Levi's advertisement (Eureka, Utah).

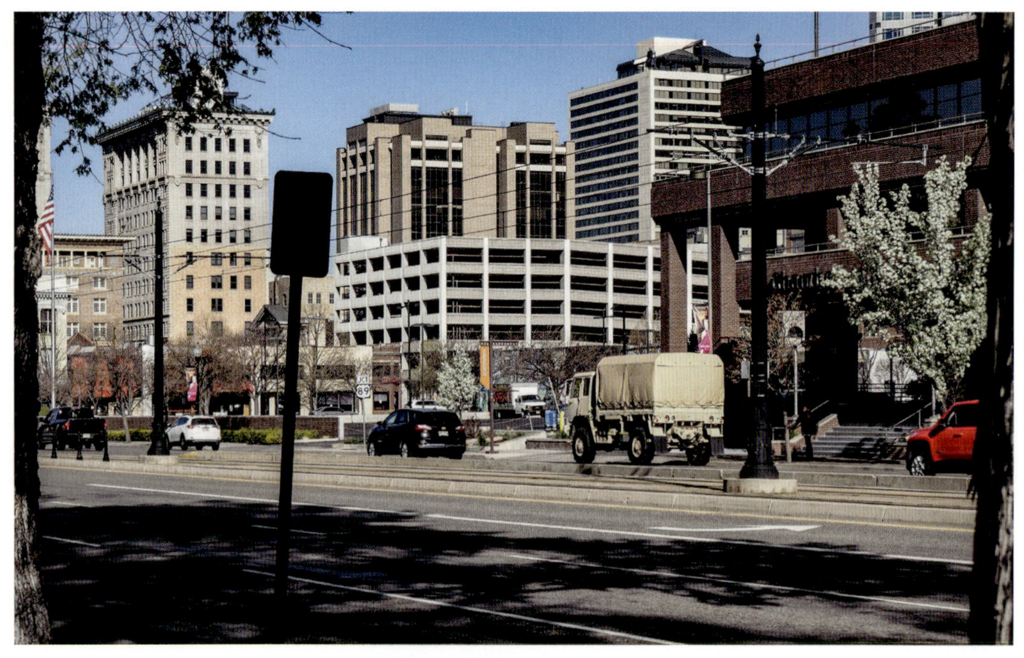

Near the time of the riots in early 2020, military vehicles were regularly seen throughout the city.

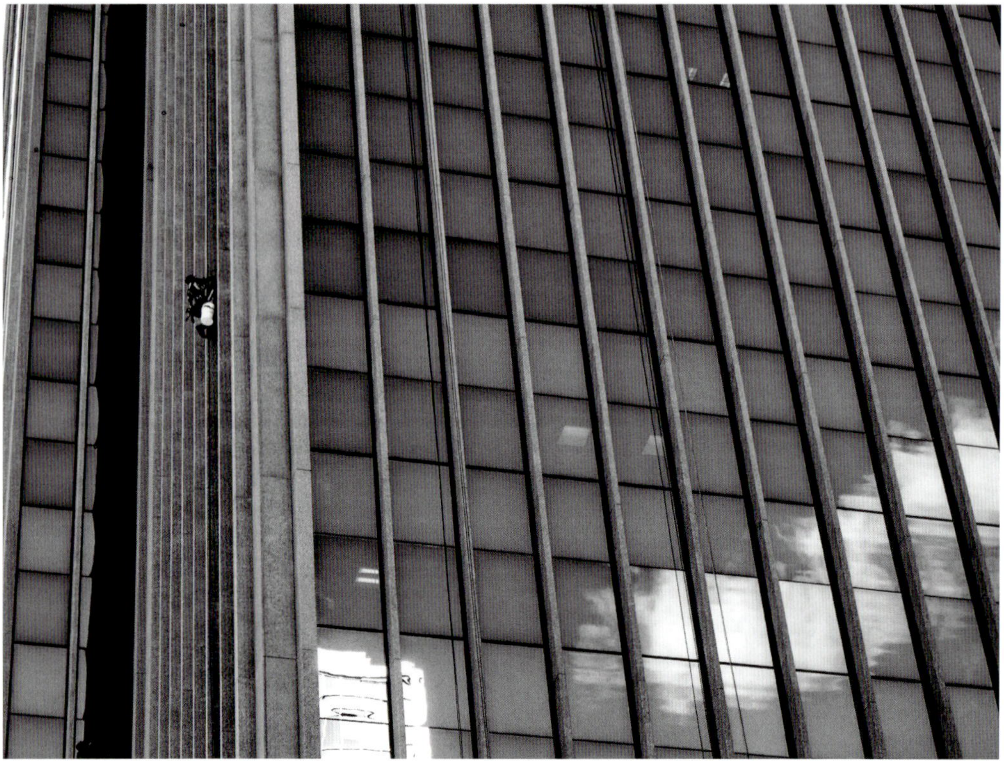

Don't look down.

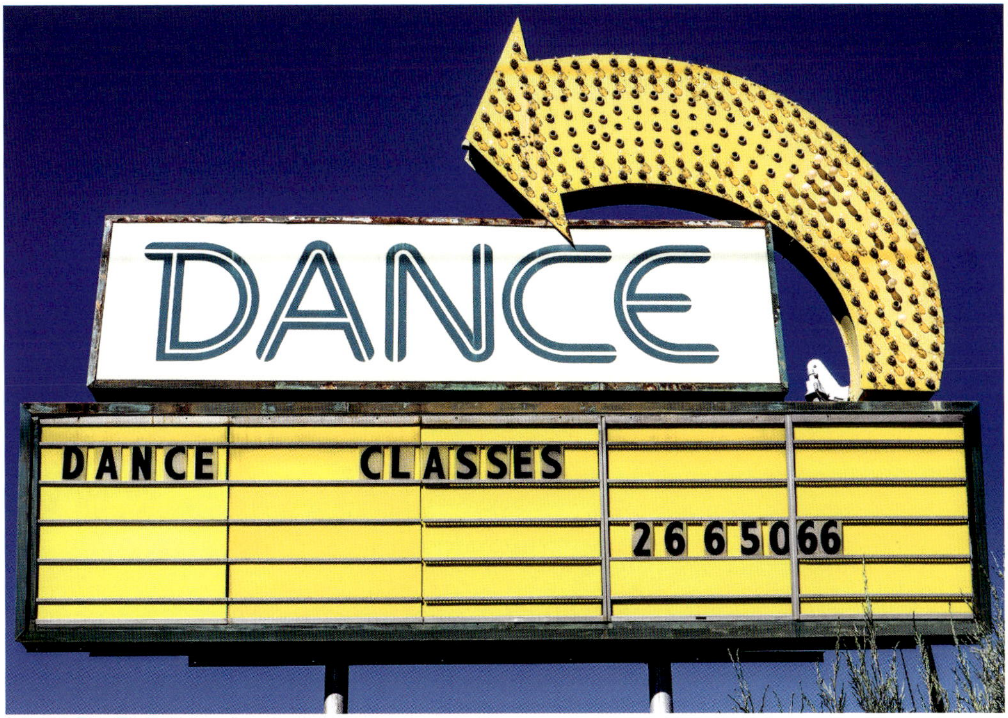

Dance the night away.

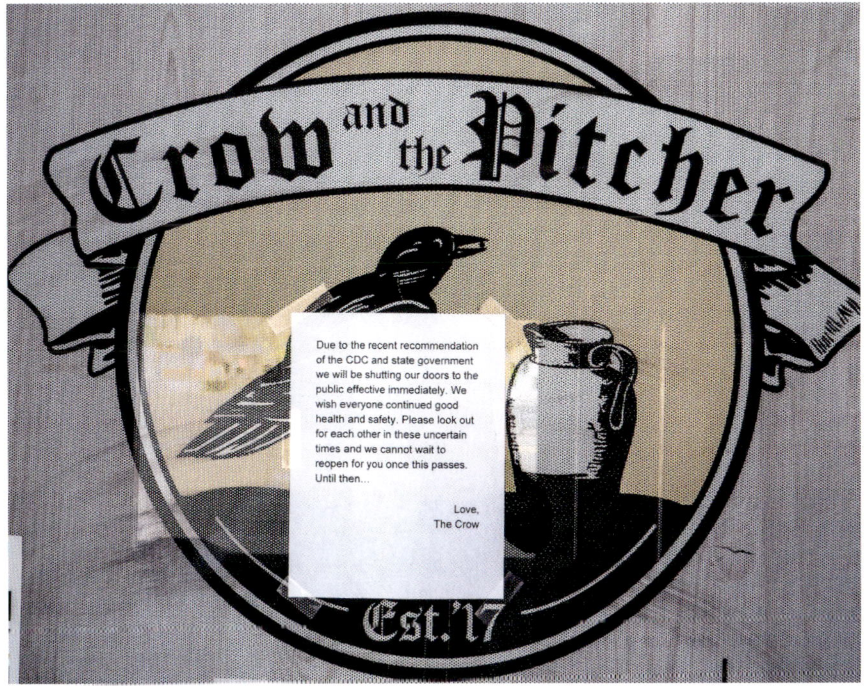

Temporarily closed due to Covid.

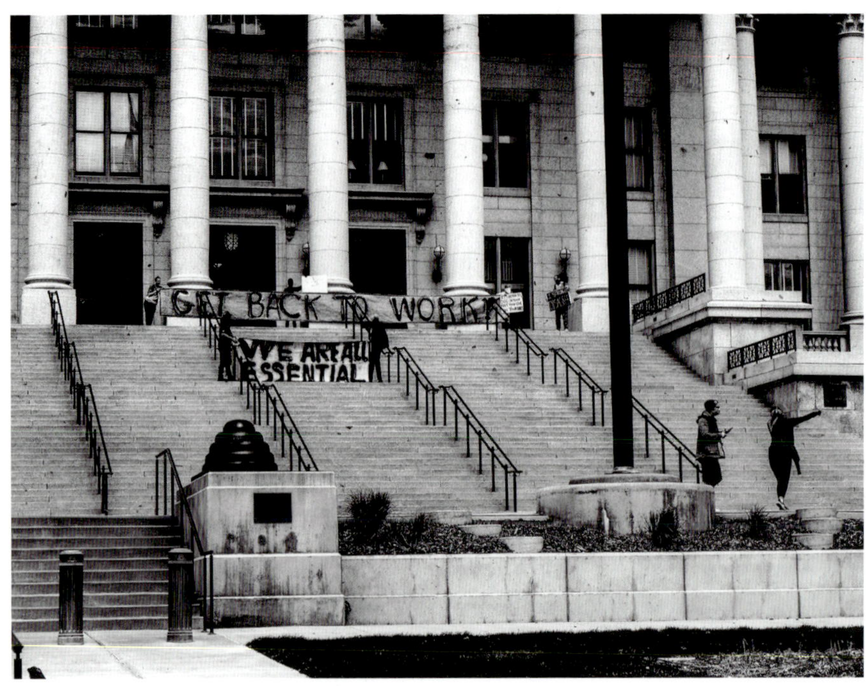

Anti-shutdown protesters occupy the steps of the Utah state capitol building.

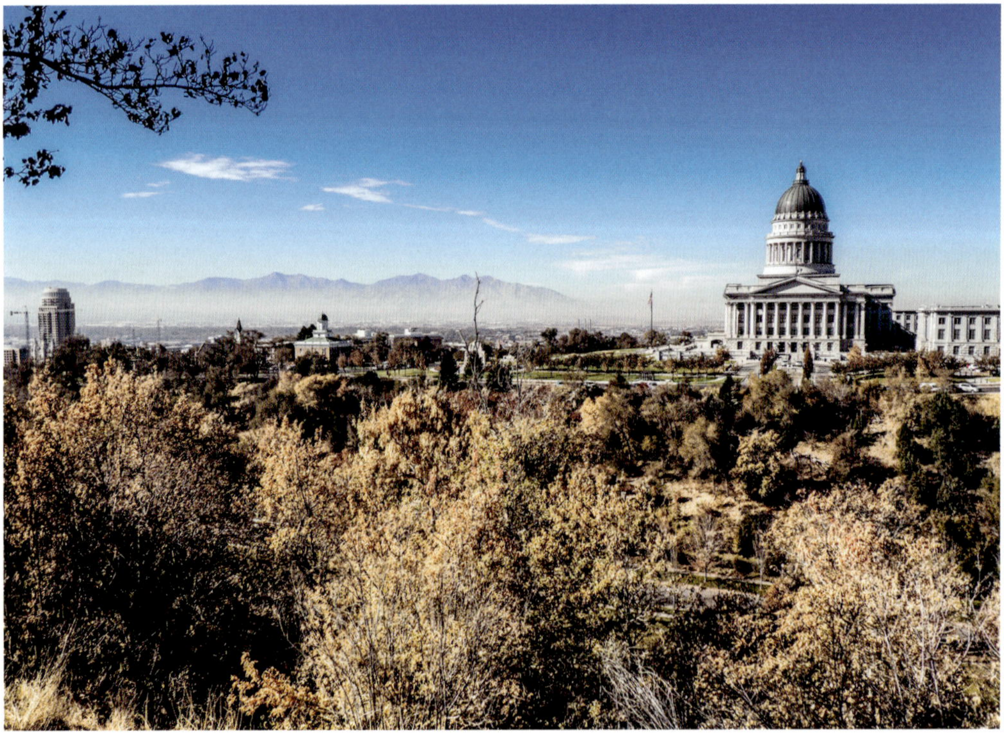

Fall views.

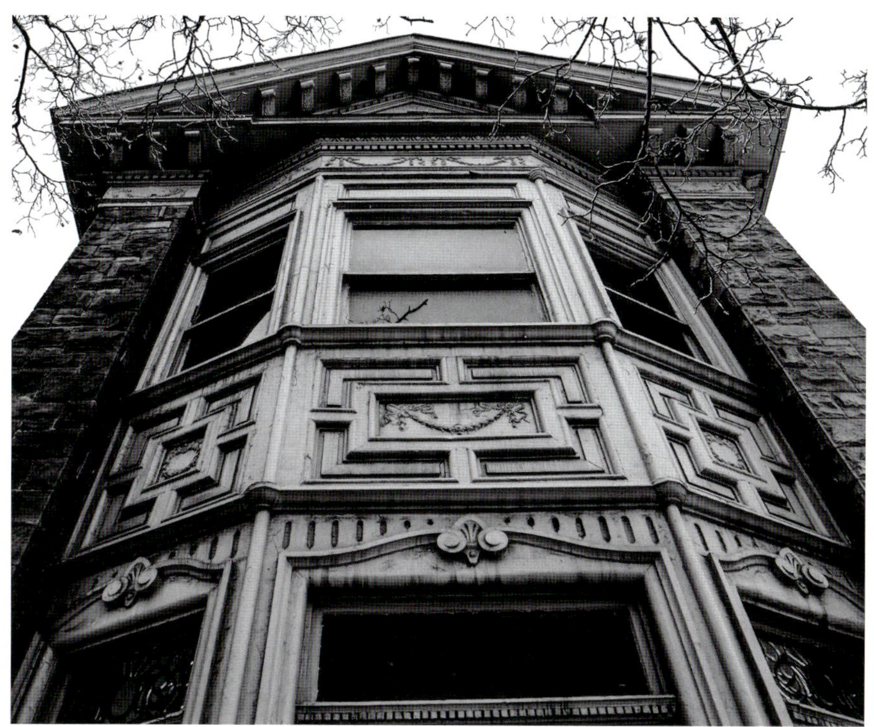

Salt Lake is full of beautiful abandoned structures.

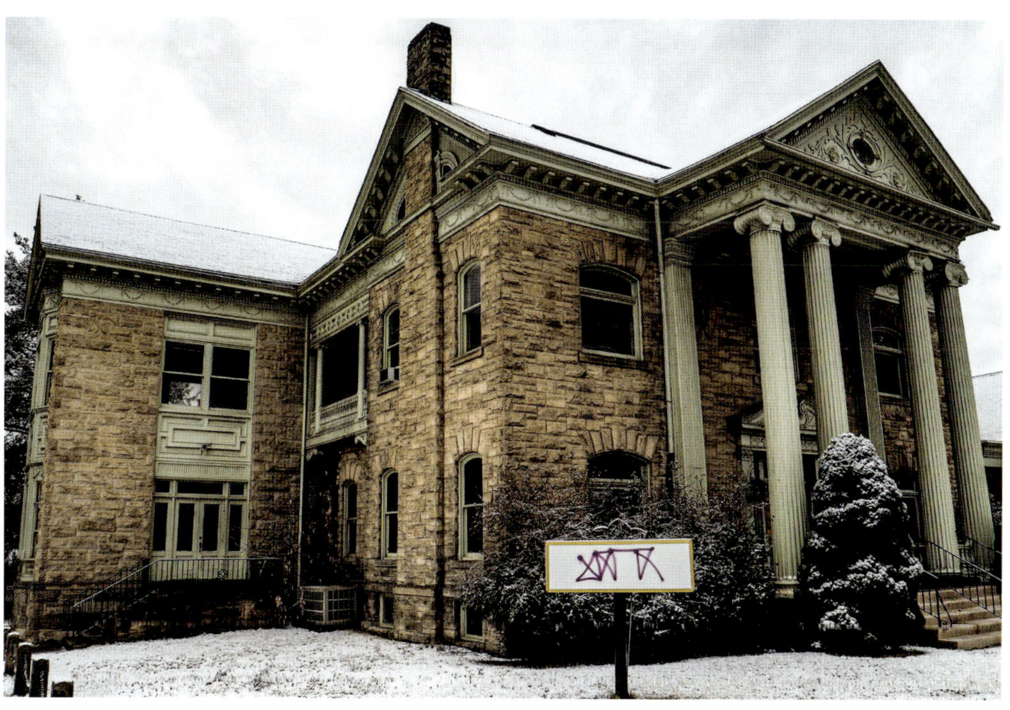

Abandoned mortuary.

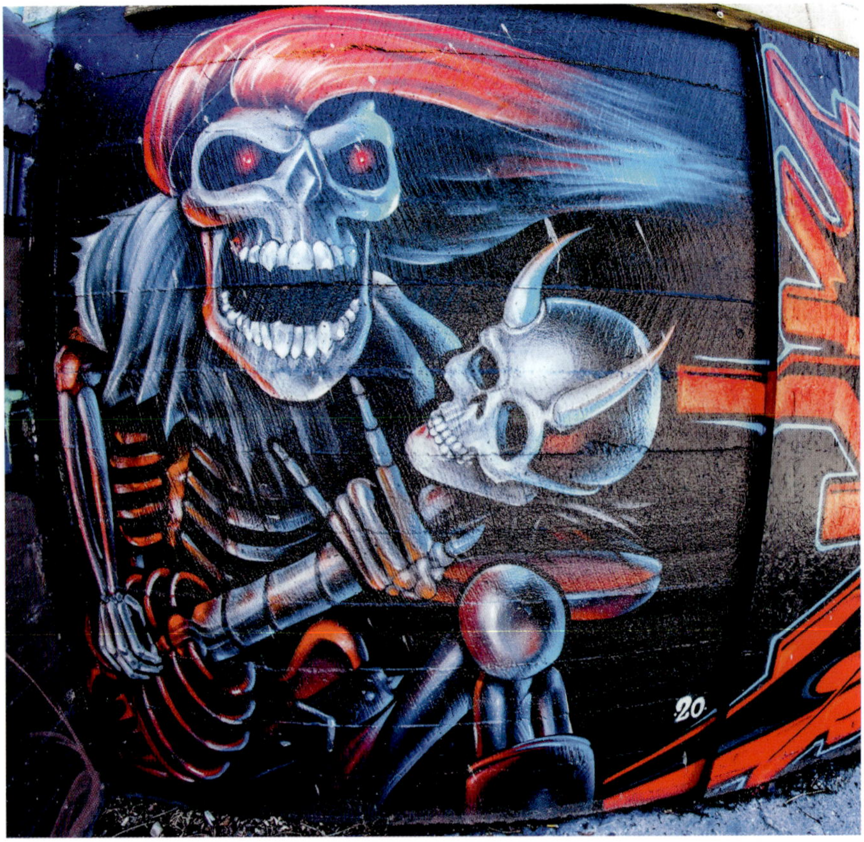

A spectacular example of urban art.

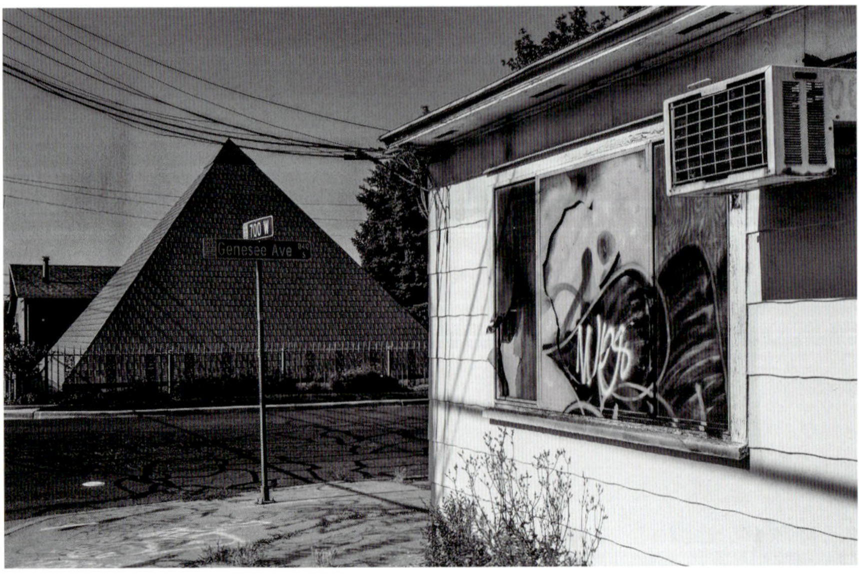

Summum pyramid.

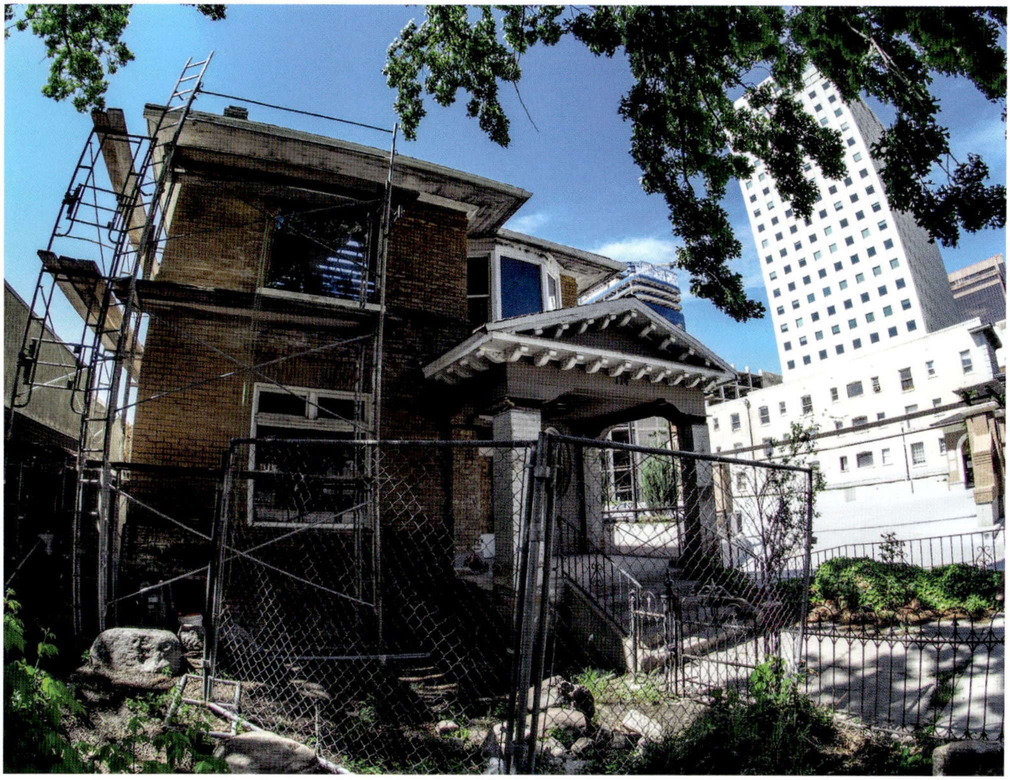

Struck by fire, the historic home of Heber J. Grant is now being restored.

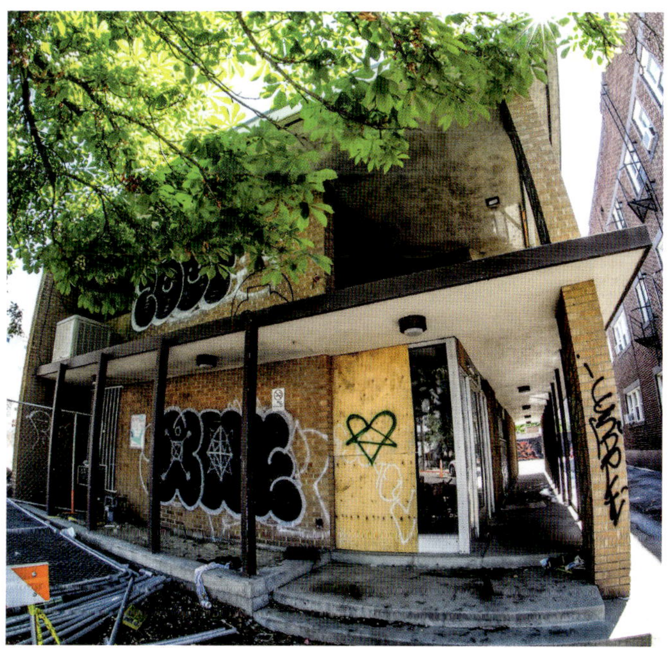

Zoot.

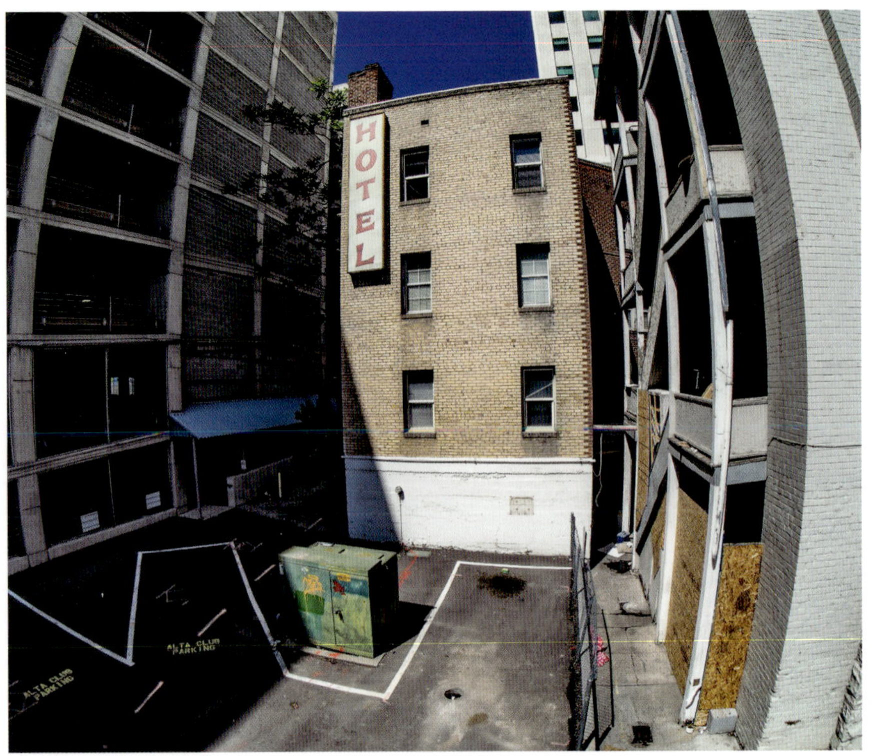

Back alley hotel.

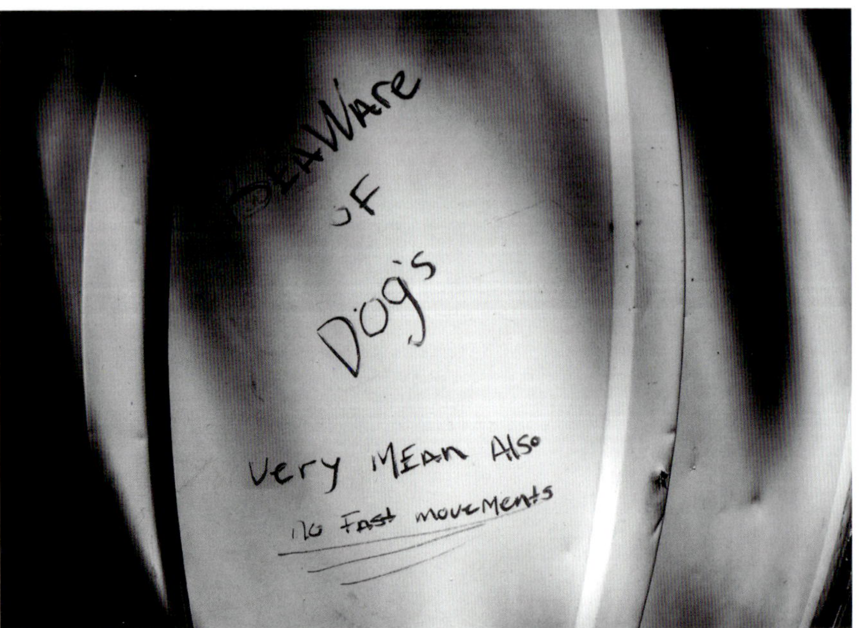

No fast movements!

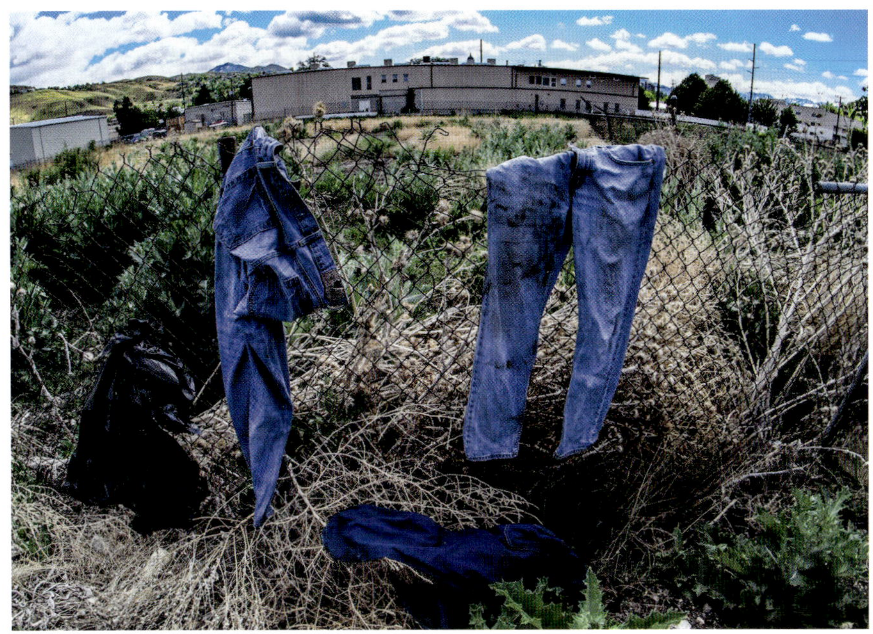

Air dry.

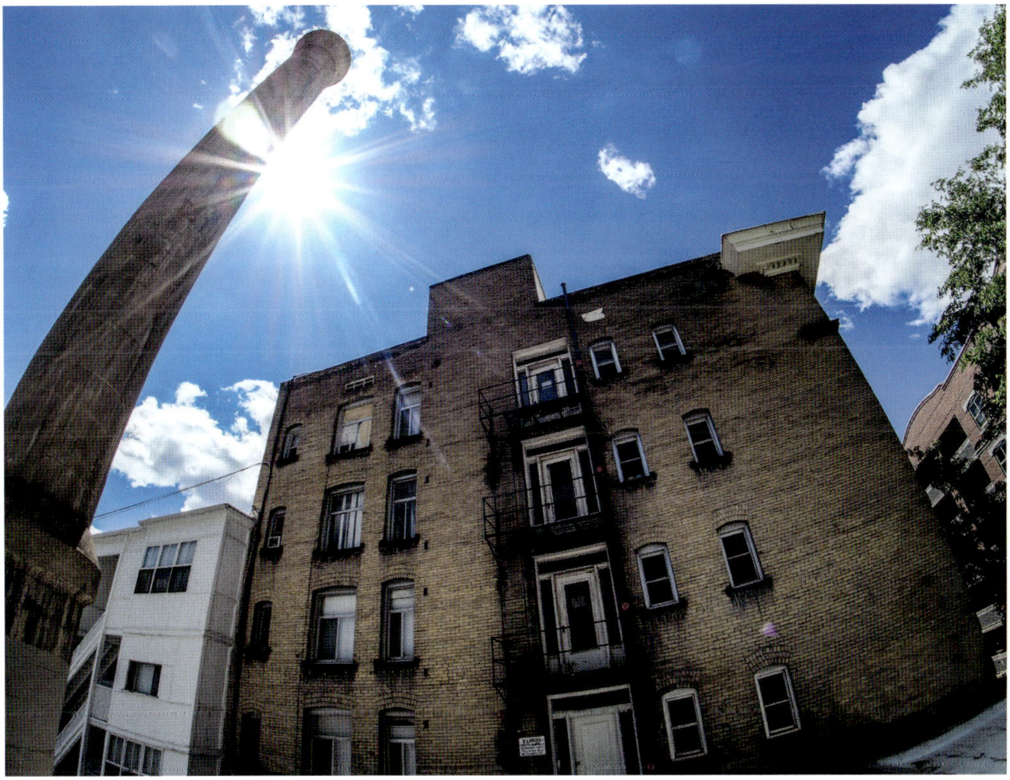

Life through my lens can be a little distorted.

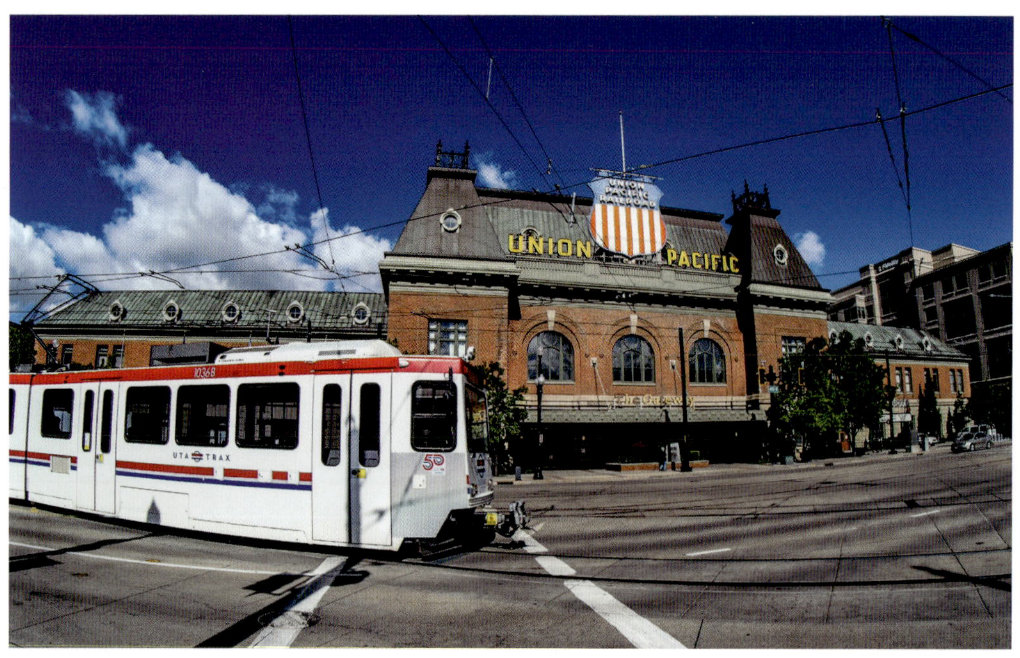

Union Pacific meets UTA.

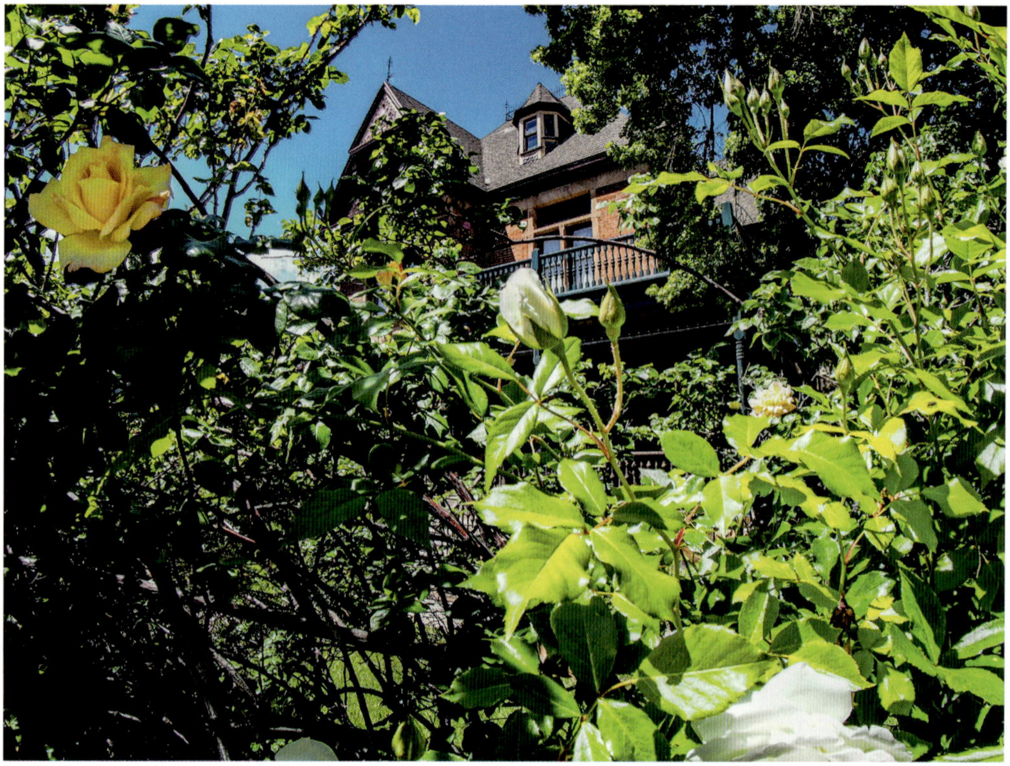

A peek through the bushes.

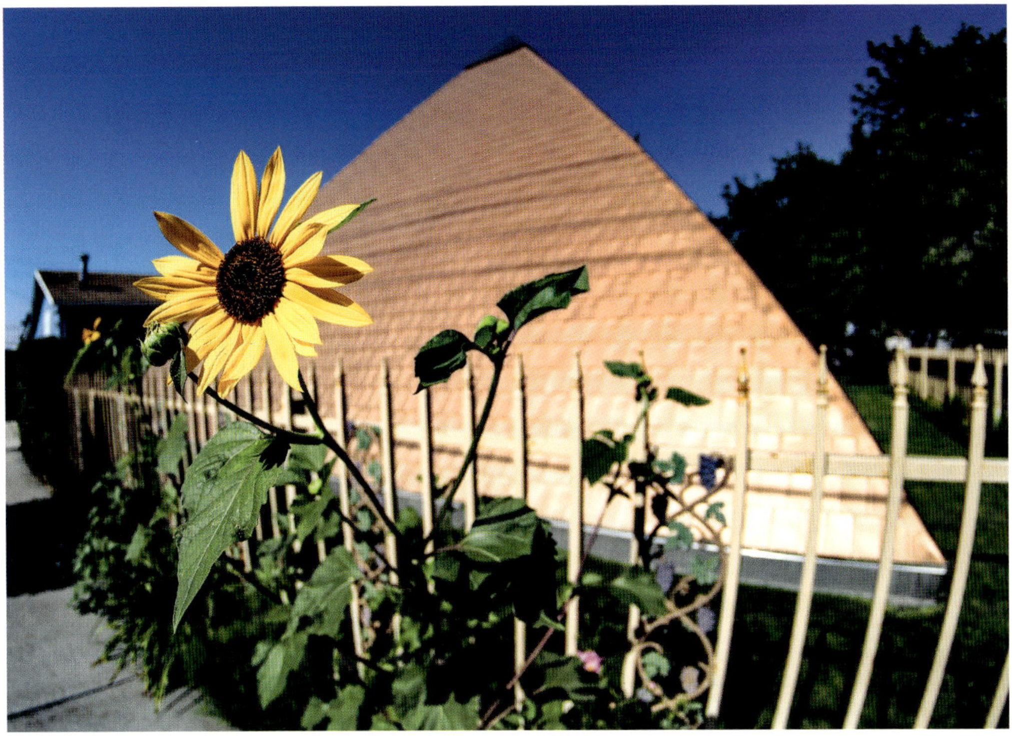

Summum sunflower.

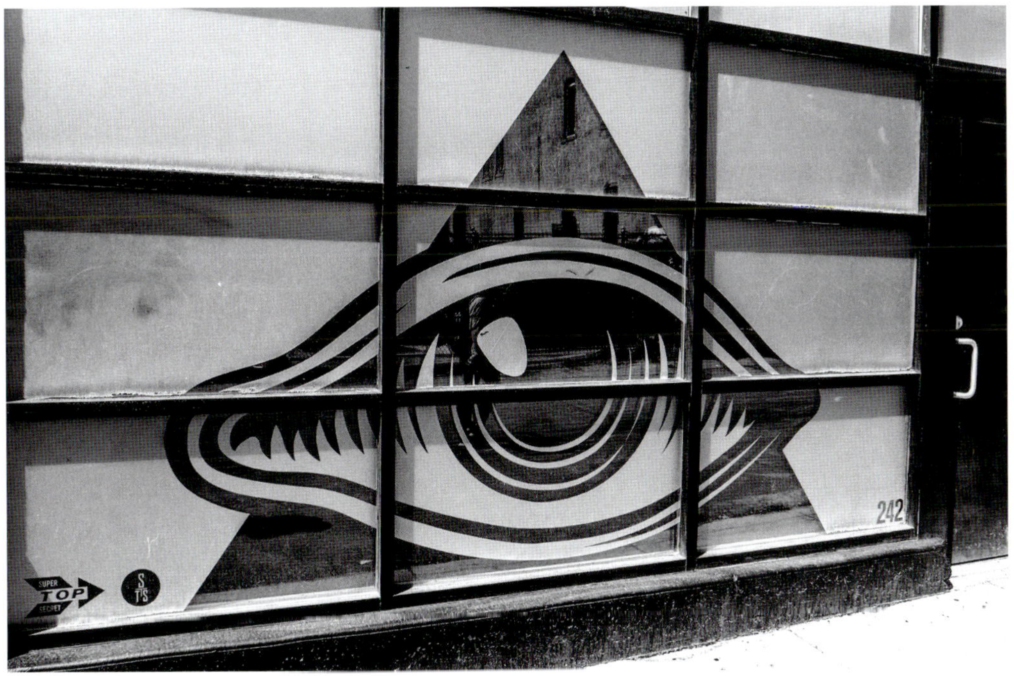

They're watching you.

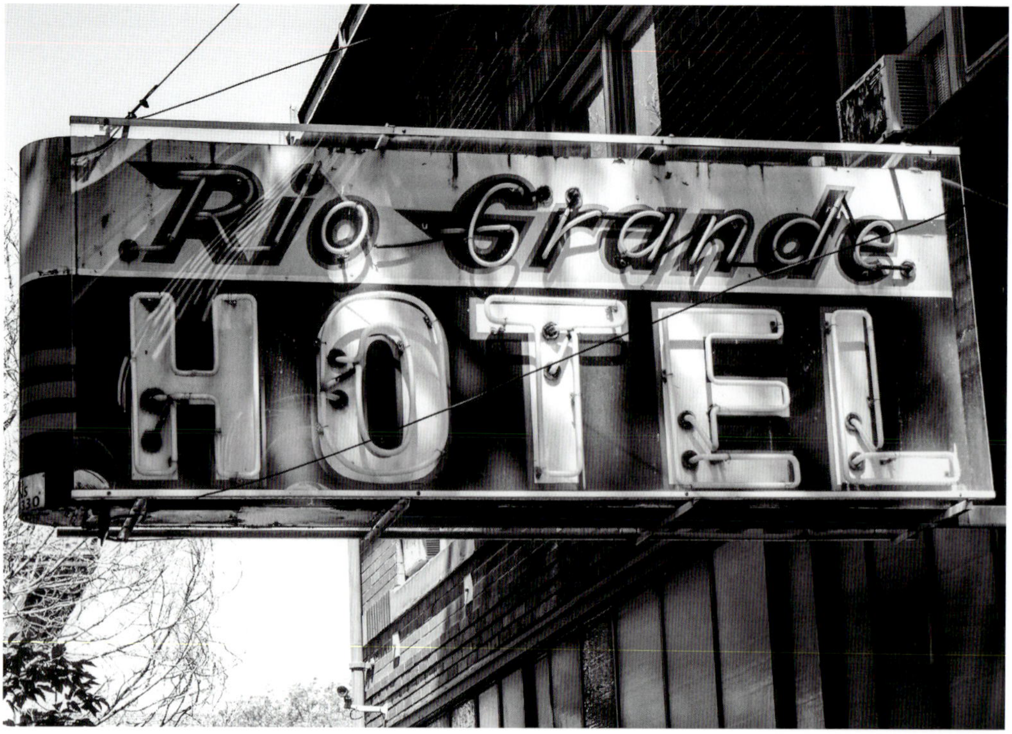

Rio Grande Hotel.

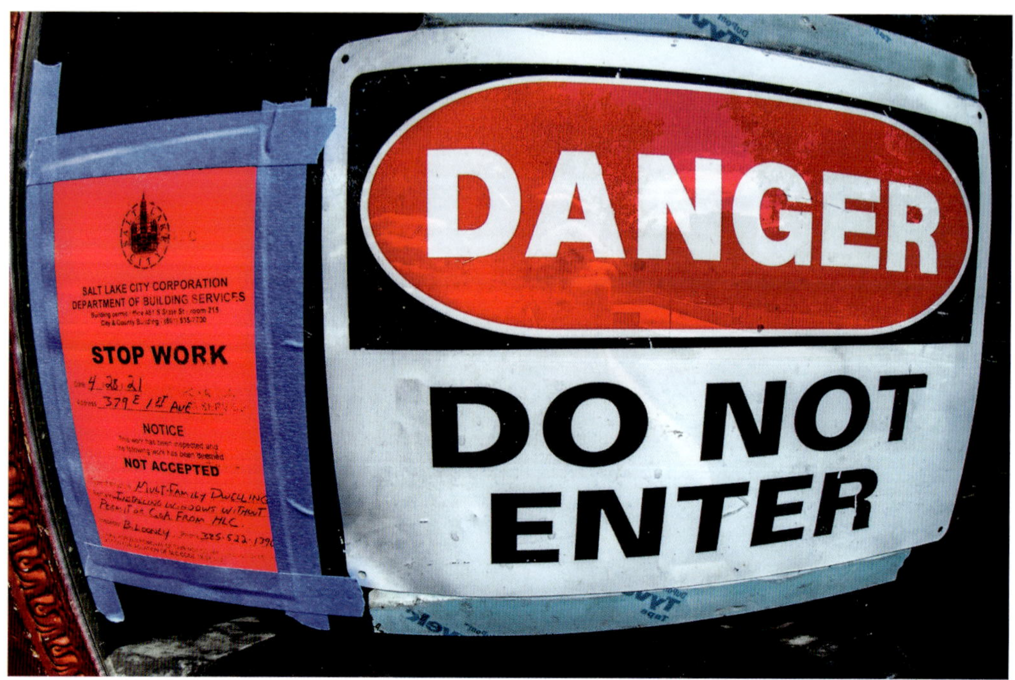

Do not enter!

Bibliography

"Gilgal." Gilgal Sculpture Garden, gilgalgarden.org/about-gilgal-sculpture-garden/.

"Haunted Places in Salt Lake City, UT." Haunted Rooms America, 3 Feb. 2020, hauntedrooms.com/utah/salt-lake-city/haunted-places.

God Squad Rabbi Marc Gellman & Monsignor Thomas Hartman. "Honoring Dead with Pebbles on Tombstones." Sun, 15 Sept. 2018, sun-sentinel.com/news/fl-xpm-2006-07-29-0607270825-story.html#:~:text=Since%20then%2C%20setting%20tombstones%20over,grave%20of%20their%20loved%20one.

"International Peace Gardens ." International Peace Gardens Academy-Jordan Park, Salt Lake City, Utah, USA, internationalpeacegardens.org/.

Jones, Jennifer. "Lilly Gray: Victim of the Beast 666." The Dead History, 23 Sept. 2019, thedeadhistory.com/lilly-gray-victim-of-the-beast-666-2/.

"McCune Mansion." Haunted Houses, 11 June 2021, hauntedhouses.com/utah/mccune-mansion/.

"McCune Mansion." Utah Historical Markers, utahhistoricalmarkers.org/c/slc/mccune-mansion/.

"Our Role in History." Our Role in History - Alta Club, altaclub.org/Default.aspx?p=DynamicModule&pageid=386318&ssid=305746&vnf=1.

"Our Story." McCune Mansion, 1 Jan. 2021, mccunemansion.com/our-story/.

Parshall, Ardis E. "Emo's Grave." *The Salt Lake Tribune*, archive.sltrib.com/story.php?ref=%2Fnews%2Fci_12815178.

SLCtvmedia. "Salt Lake City History - Fisher Mansion." YouTube, 5 Feb. 2015, youtube.com/watch?v=CEXAzNYKZao.

Smart, Christopher. "Whatever Happened to FISHER BREWERY?" *The Salt Lake Tribune*, 2016, archive.sltrib.com/article.php?id=4270530&itype=CMSID.

Southwest, The American. "Cisco." The American Southwest, americansouthwest.net/utah/cisco/index.html#:~:text=The%20tiny%20settlement%20of%20Cisco,steam%20trains%20by%20diesel%20engines.

Ugc. "Summum Pyramid." Atlas Obscura, 2 July 2010, www.atlasobscura.com/places/summum-pyramid.

Ugc. "Victim of the Beast Gravestone." Atlas Obscura, 22 Feb. 2012, www.atlasobscura.com/places/lily-e-gray-victim-of-the-beast-666-gravestone.

"Utah's Hidden Secret: Gilgal Sculpture Garden." Salt Lake City Hotels, Restaurants, Events, Things to Do & Shopping, Visit Salt Lake, 26 June 2018, www.visitsaltlake.com/blog/stories/post/utahs-hidden-secret-gilgal-sculpture-garden/.

Wiersdorf, G. William. "Masonic Temple." History of The Masonic Temple in Salt Lake City, Utah, onlineutah.us/masonictemplehistory.shtml.

www.facebook.com/leiainthefield. "Run Down Waterpark." *The Salt Lake Tribune*, 30 Oct. 2020, www.sltrib.com/news/politics/2020/10/30/salt-lake-city-wants/.

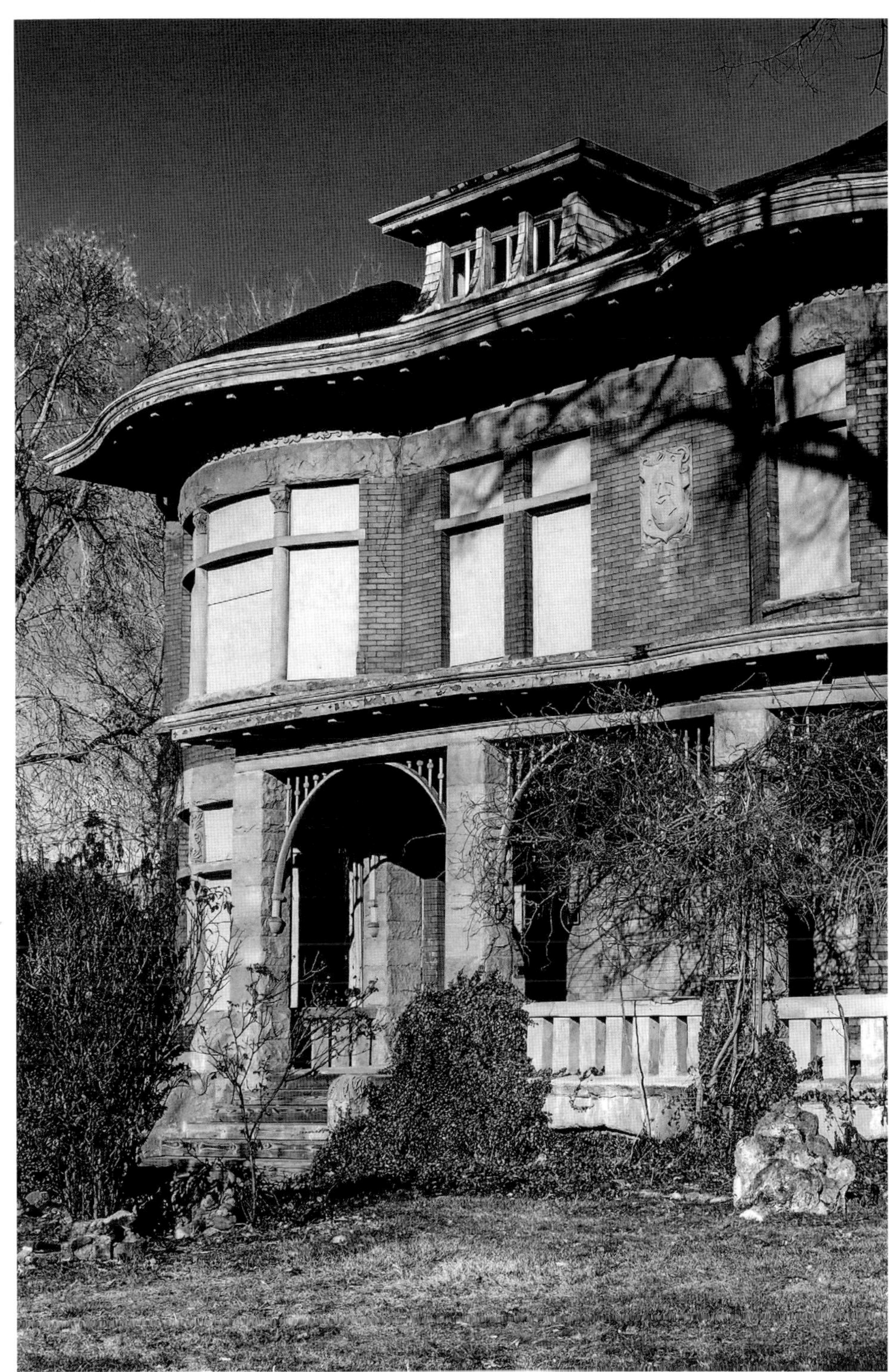

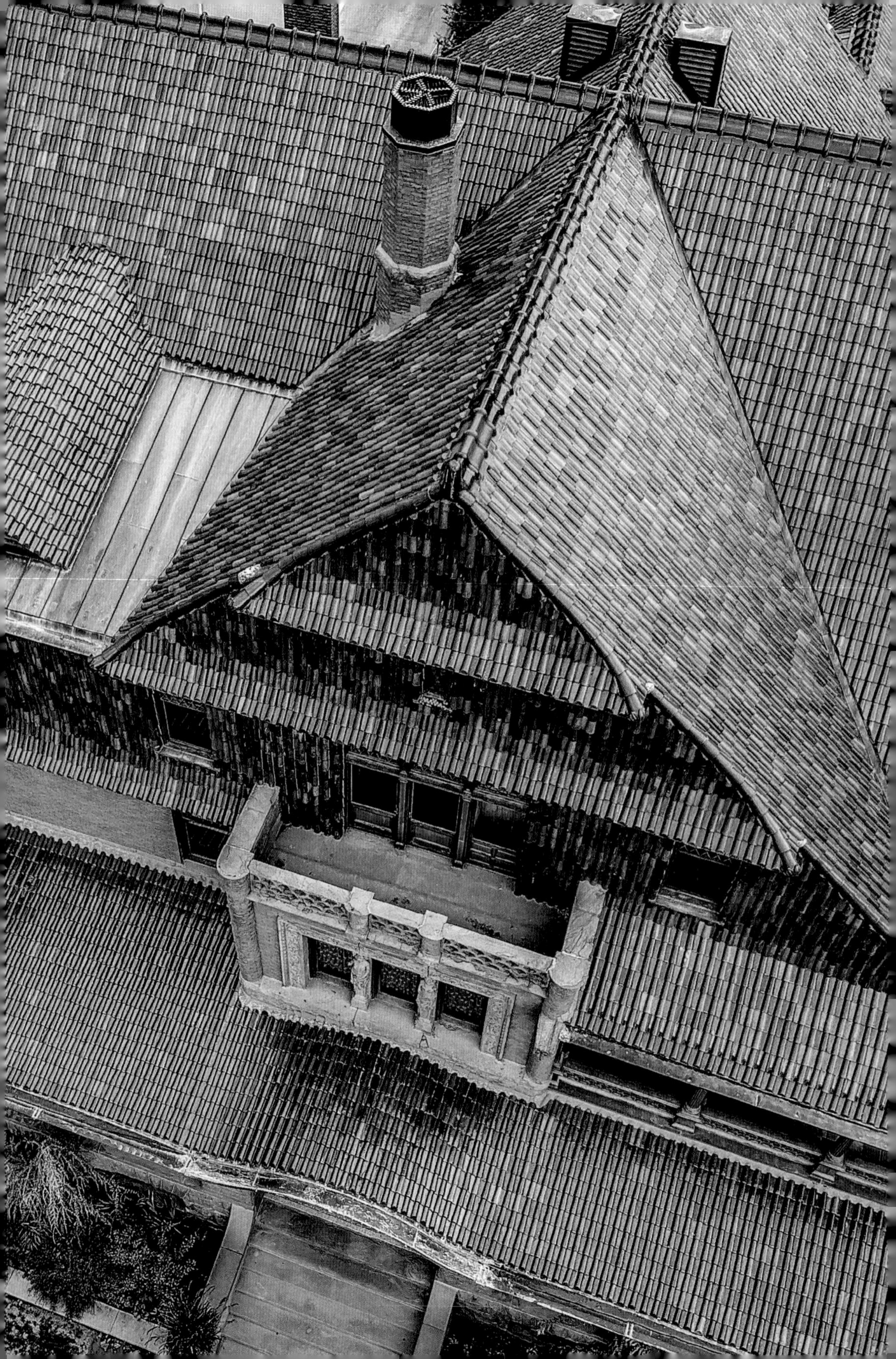